holy parenting:

MAKING THE COMMON SACRED

BENJAMIN KERNS

holy parenting:
MAKING THE COMMON SACRED

BENJAMIN KERNS

dedication:

This book is dedicated to my amazing wife, who is my dearest friend and partner. I am the person, parent, and pastor I am because of your love and grace. Thank you for encouraging me to love Jesus and our kids with all my heart!

TABLE OF CONTENTS

Introduction: Moving Past The Christmas Photo Veneer   6

Part One: Accepting Your New Life   12
Chapter 1:   We Are Not in Kansas Anymore   13
Chapter 2:   Your Old Life is Over   20
Chapter 3:   The Death of Quiet Time   30
Chapter 4:   The Stakes Could Not Be Higher   38
Chapter 5:   What Needs to Change? (Me, My Expectations, or My Worldview?)   46

Part Two: Raising Little Children is a Spiritual Discipline.   55
Chapter 1:   The Presence; an Introduction   56
Chapter 2:   Breakfast: the Most Important Meal of the Day   64
Chapter 3:   Building Blocks and Tea Parties: The Ministry of Play   72
Chapter 4:   Play Dates: the Fertile Ground of Community   80
Chapter 5:   Nap Time: Needed Rest For Everyone!   88
Chapter 6:   Car Time: Keeping the Conversation Going   95
Chapter 7:   Stranger Danger: Developing Discernment   103
Chapter 8:   Say No to Facebook: a Needed Fast.   111
Chapter 9:   Scrapbooking: the Oldest Spiritual Discipline   119
Chapter 10:   Bedtime: Reshaping the Day   128
Chapter 11:   Midnight Mayhem: Though I Walk Through the Valley, You Are With Me   137
Chapter 12:   "I Will Never": A Lifestyle of Teachability   146

Part Three: Vital Rhythms for Spiritual Growth.   155
Chapter 1:   You Can't Pass on What You Don't Have   156
Chapter 2:   Reengaging in Corporate Worship   165
Chapter 3:   Putting the "School" Back in Sunday   175
Chapter 4:   Bible Studies and Billiards   183
Chapter 5:   Attempting the Family Devotional   192

Conclusion: Confessions of an Average Dad   200

Acknowledgements   205

About the Author   208

introduction: MOVING PAST THE CHRISTMAS PHOTO VENEER

What is Behind That Perfect Christmas Card of Yours?

It is once again that special, all-important time of year. It is time to gather the family together, coordinate our clothing and bust out the family Christmas photo. It is our one time to pose for the defining picture of our family that will reveal how perfect our family is to our friends and relatives.

This is the picture that shows off how much we love each other, how well-mannered our kids are, and what nice smiles they have. Our family is so perfect that even the dog will just sit there and pose in front of the camera, waiting patiently for us all to smile and not blink. Our Christmas photo is the summation of the year and, as if by a miracle from God, every year ends on a great note, with everyone in our family smiling, hoping to be placed on your fridge.

When we were first married, the Christmas photo was a fun exercise for my wife and I. We went to a nice location, had a friend take a couple of pics. We enjoyed having up-to-date pictures of us, so in love and enjoying life to share. But soon our friends started adding children to their Christmas photos. And their families matched so well and their kids were so well-behaved.

After reading their Christmas letters we saw their children weren't just physically beautiful and perfectly behaved, but brilliant and clever as well. At first we were thrilled God was so gracious to our friends. But when it became our turn to have children and include them in the Christmas photo, I realized our family could never compete.

In an attempt to stay on par with our peers, we decided to include our kids in our annual photo. But if you look closer at our picture you would be able see that everything is not quite what it seems. At first you might miss it because my wife is so beautiful, or because my kids are so cute, but look closer. Even if you look at my face you might still miss it because I am sporting such a big smile. But if you studied at my eyes, the eyes behind the big smile, behind the perfectly behaved family you will see frustration on the brink of rage.

This is because this picture does not tell the entire story, this picture shows the story we want to tell our friends and family, the story of how great our family is, how in love we are, how well-behaved and brilliant our children are. It is just a snapshot designed to prove to ourselves that we are a happy well-adjusted family.

If you were at our house during the hour-long fiasco that was our Christmas photo, this is what you would have experienced: Me, rushing home from work only to have an hour to change, pose for the pictures, eat dinner, and head back to work for a very important meeting. I pulled into the driveway expecting my family to be all on the same page as me. I had one hour. As I opened he door my son was jumping on the couch, my daughter just pooped through her diaper and my wife hadn't even changed yet.

But have no fear, "kind and patient dad" just got home. Oh wait, wrong dad.

I immediately got into bossy mode, barking orders and asking unhelpful rhetorical questions. After 20 minutes of chaos we were all dressed and ready for our picture. *Remember we're a loving and happy family, so wipe those tears away and get the dog to face forward!* Miracle of all miracles we had it in only three tries. Oh wait--the person using the camera didn't realize that there needed to be a flash; that pitch black and blurry one was not the kind of photo we were going for.

Five more minutes in and my daughter started to lose it. We passed her around making silly faces, bribing her with food, anything to get her to smile even for a second. But with all this commotion, our dog got nervous and started to walk away, then wouldn't face the same way. I could feel this great family moment slipping away. After another ten minutes we came back together, daughter calmed down, dog facing the right way, flash on. So close!

But by this point my son was totally over the family photo and wanted to use the opportunity to show off his amazing collection of silly faces. It was a science, smiling like a good boy until the very last second where he would contort his face, stick out his tongue and do some strange thing with his hands. This was the end of the rope for me. Time-outs were issued, firm words spoken, blood boiling. I knew there was no dinner for me tonight and any hope of the Kerns' house having a Christmas photo worth mailing out was slipping away.

With minutes remaining we grouped up one more time and snapped off a few last pictures. With stern warnings and the reminder of how fun this was and how much we loved each other we all smiled. Sure enough we got one photo that would serve as our annual family Christmas photo, the photo that showed off how much we love each other, how well behaved our kids were, and what an amazing year we'd had.

Where is Real Life Found?

For me, the experience of gathering for a family photo has proven to be the ultimate example of how pictures don't seem to always capture real life. The Christmas photo is a manufactured event for a very small moment in time. But what I have noticed about myself, and some of my friends, is that we're living a life for those contrived moments, and are missing the real life that happens along the way.

We've mastered the art of presentation and in the process are totally missing an opportunity for a real encounter--a real encounter with one another, and a real encounter with the living God who created us in His image, who designed the family and desires to walk with us in all of this.

Before kids everything was great. We were in control. We had all the time in the world to work, exercise, read, pray, laugh, play... How amazing Saturday mornings were with my wife! We would sleep in, eventually get up and go to Starbucks with our Bibles, journal, and newspaper. We would spend an hour or two just loving each other, loving Jesus, reflecting on how blessed we were. If we wanted to grow spiritually, it was as simple as making some time before work, after work, Saturday morning, whenever. In fact, I would get double points for including my wife in this endeavor.

After kids, it is all over. Try telling your husband when he gets home from work that you need him to watch the kids and make dinner so you can get some alone-time and refresh spiritually, praying God would grow your heart for Him and your kids. Or vise versa: if you are the husband, try calling your wife who's been home with the kids all day, and let her know you'll be home an hour late so you can get some "me" time to unwind and reflect on all that God is doing in your life and family.

This is a recipe for disaster. This new life is full of unexpected chaos where every sense of personal space and boundaries are under assault. It is finally becoming clear--your life is no longer your own. Whatever space there is gets swallowed up with laundry, cleaning, shopping, and then *maybe* sitting on the couch with your spouse. Within this new rhythm of life, which is actually no rhythm of life, finding space to be fed spiritually, to grow deeper in faith, to be so connected to God so that the fruit of the Spirit is overflowing, is becoming a distant memory.

This chaotic season of raising little kids doesn't have to be a spiritual desert. In fact, this particular time of life can actually be one of spiritual renewal, as you are being stretched in brand new ways and potentially growing deeper by leaps and bounds. God is love. He made us and loves us. He created the process of childbirth and child-rearing.

By readjusting or patterns of spiritual growth and disciplines there is a real opportunity for God to do brand new things in the heart of you and your family. The truth is that God is alive and active during every phase of life. Wherever God is active and at work is a holy place.

Maybe the gentle grace that God has for you is to stop working so hard for these picture perfect moments to show off your family and to grow in your faith. And maybe the invitation God has for you is to relax, open your eyes and see how He is actively involved in every part of your day making the most common things sacred.

Every transition of life stage forces us to mature and adapt, when we were kids, adolescents, young adults, college students, young marrieds, and now parents of little ones. Instead of being crushed by guilt and shame for not being able to get up and shower and have a quiet time before your kids wake up at 6:00, maybe it's time to stop and ask God what sort of new rhythms of relationship and growth He is inviting you into. I am confident that this season of raising little children is not at odds with growing spiritually. In fact, I'm convinced that the very act of raising children can and should be a spiritual discipline.

My prayer for you and your family as well as for me and mine, is that:

"God would give us eyes to see and ears to hear the incredible adventure we have been invited to participate in. As we become more like Jesus and give our lives away to our children, we will grow in grace and love and model to our children, family, friends and neighbors, the joy of living a real and authentic life that is full of grace and peace. May we give up the false veneer of perfection and see how God is transforming the common into the sacred."

Let the adventure begin!

section one:
ACCEPTING YOUR NEW LIFE

chapter one: YOU ARE NOT IN KANSAS ANYMORE

I Love The Wizard of Oz

As you can already tell, traditions, whether formal or informal, are an important part of family life for me. One of my favorite family traditions growing up was watching The Wizard of Oz with my cousins on Thanksgiving. It wasn't so much the movie itself that was so great, but it was what piling onto a couch with my family, eating a bowl of popcorn, and singing all the songs came to mean.

Because our extended family was spread out, we were rarely all in the same place at the same time. Thanksgiving became the one time a year when we would all be together. The adults would cook and enjoy wine while the kids would play games and occasionally, get into trouble. With the football game as the soundtrack and the aroma of turkey filling the home, my cousins and I would create elaborate plays and choreographed dances to perform. As the football games ended, it was time for the show. While the appetizers were served, my cousins and I would perform our annual play complete with costumes, song and dance. Our parents beamed with pride as we got dressed up and sang our guts out. Once the show was over it was time to eat. And boy, did we eat!

Because I was a kid, I didn't really pay attention to the adult time around the table. My cousins and I would scarf down our food and then ask to be excused so we could watch movies. Without fail, the same movie was selected year after year. It was a VHS tape recording of *Airplane* followed by The Wizard of Oz. After 10 years of this rhythm, The Wizard of Oz has come to be pregnant with memories and emotion. It has come to represent the best of times for my family and my childhood.

Recently, The Wizard of Oz came on TV, and I was excited to watch it again with my own family. After a great dinner together, we put the kids in their pajamas, and I made popcorn. We then all climbed onto the couch and my heart was full of anticipation for the joy to pass down one of my favorite family traditions to my own kids. Sitting there together, my heart was momentarily warm with the idea of being together as a family, enjoying an amazing movie. But as the movie dragged on and my kids were scared of the witch and the flying monkeys, my attempt at family bonding unraveled into a tornado of chaos and crying. It would be great if I had been a whole enough person to understand that this movie might be a little above my two- and five-year-old, and that a movie made over 70 years ago might not be relevant to the Sesame Street generation. I was hurt and disappointed at my complete strikeout, so I sent the kids to bed. A better choice would probably have been to be gracious and kind and throw in *A Toy Story*.

It seems like so much of my parenting is taking these glorified memories of my childhood and putting them on my own kids. When their responses don't match my idealized version, I get frustrated and angry. I wonder if part of this frustration doesn't lie in the fact that I have not fully come to terms with this new life that is unfolding before my eyes.

We Are Not in Kansas Anymore

In *The Wizard of Oz,* Dorothy's house is ripped from its foundations and sent flying through the air within a tornado only to crash land in a completely new environment, one full of color, mystery, surprise, and uncertainty. She used to live in Kansas on a tiny farm where everything was in black and white, but now she finds her self firmly planted in the "wonderful" world of Oz. Oz is completely different from her homeland.

This world was filled with little people with funny voices, witches, talking scarecrows, and random singing (okay, the random singing happened in her old world, too). Smart girl that she was, Dorothy realized immediately that "...we're not in Kansas anymore!" She knew that this world was not her home; she decided she was going to do everything in her power to get back to her old life. With fixed resolve, she put on the ruby slippers and began down the yellow brick road that would lead her to her old life and familiar rhythms.

In a similar way, the second our child is born, we have come to realize that we too are now in a completely foreign world. Before our baby arrived, it was easy to imagine all the upside a child would bring to our lives and to our families. But this fantasy has now come to a screeching halt. Our house has just crash landed in Oz and we must get our bearings and come up with a plan! We are suddenly overwhelmed by all that is in front of us; little people with funny voices, sleepless nights, screaming and throw-up, and almost no spontaneous singing. Soon it becomes clear: we are definitely not in Kansas anymore.

Dorothy spent all her time and effort in Oz trying to return to her former life. And although there were many trials and disappointments, Dorothy did finally wake up from her dream of Oz to find herself back in Kansas. As our babies grow and scream and cry, and we get little sleep, and our former friends want less and less to do with us, the thought soon crosses our mind that it might be nice to find some ruby slippers, get on that yellow brick road, and head back to Kansas. But the truth is, Dorothy's path cannot be our path.

We Can't Go Back

The reality is we have kids. This is not a dream. This is the world we now live in, and as much as we sometimes want to, we can never go back. Wanting to go back doesn't mean that you don't love your child or that you regret the decision to have her. But raising kids isn't easy, and wanting to go back is a normal thought we must contend with and work through. This "wonderful" world of Oz is our new reality, and we can either make the best of it, or we can spend an entire season of our lives being disheartened and depressed, wishing we were back in Kansas. Since we find ourselves in Oz, we actually have three distinct choices in front of us.

What Are My Options?

One choice is to pretend that we didn't really land in a strange and different world. We actually aren't in Oz, we have just stumbled into a Baby Gap. We can try to keep up the same rhythms that we always have without missing a beat. Our little guys are small and cute, we can take them with us, we can take them out to restaurants and even to movies. We think that this addition to our families won't actually change how we live our lives, and that we will never own a minivan. This is a choice and one that most of us make at first. But as our kids grow and develop, it will take more and more effort to try to live the pre-kid lifestyle. Sooner or later, we will have to come to terms with the fact that we are truly in a new world. Which leads me to the second choice.

The second choice is the easiest one to realize. This is the choice of recognizing that we have landed in a new world. The idealized dream of having kids was not even close to the land of reality. The screaming, the puking, the chaos to your health, and the natural rhythms of life you used to enjoy are too much to take. It is easy to lock it down and try to grind it out until they are old enough to be potty trained, go to preschool, in school all day, graduate from high school, have college paid for.

Bitterness is the marker of this season; a hopeless understanding that the old life is gone, and this new one is not quite what we expected. It becomes more and more easy to give up, both emotionally and physically. This leaves many people is a state of limbo as they grieve the loss of their old patterns of life and are paralyzed as they wait in vain for the light at the end of the tunnel to get closer and closer. This second choice only focuses on the loss of the way things were before kids and wants to simply remain in a state of suspended animation until some magical date in the future, rather than embracing what God might actually have in store for us as parents and for our children in this time. Living into this reality is our third option.

The third choice is actually the most difficult of the options in front of us. It is the difficult choice of recognizing that having a small child has completely altered your world and this is a new reality, with new rules, and new expectations, and for better or worse, we can never go back to the way things were. Rather than have bitterness and disappointment be the dominate emotions surrounding this truth, I want to do the hard work personally to come to terms with this new world so that I can make the best of it, cherish it, and have every day, even the most chaotic ones be a blessing to me, to my children, and to God.

Oz is a strange new world, but it is a world full of bright color and new adventures. Sometimes I wonder why Dorothy was so eager to get back to the black and white world of Kansas. Being single-minded in her quest to return, she was not able to soak up all the mysteries and beauty Oz had to offer. In a similar way, I don't want to hold on too tightly to my old world, my old rhythms, and my old expectations only to miss out all of the great things that God has in store. The reality is that there is no yellow brick road back for us as parents. Oz is our home, and the challenge is to figure out how to live fully into it.

This third choice is the only real way forward. This will take some hard work and reflection, but I believe it is our only option. In order to recognize and accept that Oz is now our home so that we can experience satisfaction and joy as we live into our new roles as parents, we must first come to terms with the hidden grief living inside of us. Grief is normal and natural. Our old life has died; it is normal and natural to grieve. Only by acknowledging, and understanding, our grief can we begin the process of healing and acceptance. The normal pattern of the grieving process is denial, anger, bargaining, depression, and then acceptance.

Acceptance is the only healthy way forward. In order to take hold of all that God has for us in this time and season, let's realize we can't go back, do the hard work, grieve this loss, and figure out how to embrace all that this season of life has to offer.

Questions for Reflection:
1) What are a couple of things you have missed since becoming a parent?
2) What are the similarities you have noticed between Oz and this new world of parenting?
3) Which choice are you making regarding this new life? Denial, Bitterness, or Acceptance?
4) What makes acceptance such a difficult choice?

chapter two: YOUR OLD LIFE IS OVER

Oh How I Miss Saturdays

There was no alarm clock set for this morning, yet I find myself awakened by a crying baby who is ready to get out of bed and play. Now, I love my baby and I love to play with her, but this is ridiculous. 6:00 in the morning, ON A SATURDAY!?!

It's a fading memory, but there was a time in my life where I loved Saturdays with all my heart. After a long hard work week, Saturday became the day of true Sabbath rest. My wife and I would sleep in until we couldn't sleep any more. Whether we got up at 8 or 11, we didn't care, and there was no guilt about it.

When we finally got out of bed we would put on our sweats, grab our dog and take a leisurely walk to the neighborhood Starbucks. We didn't talk much, since we were still waking up. But with a few sips of our coffee and a couple of bites of our scones, we were ready to enjoy the day. We would laugh about the events of the past week, or comment on our favorite shows. Sometimes we would just sit there together, my wife reading a book and me reading the paper. This was the good life!

Oh, how I miss those Saturdays! Our biggest plans involved what fun restaurant we would go to for dinner, and the hardest decision was whether to go to the movies or rent. Our conversation would often revolve around an idealized version of our future when we would be doing all of this with a family in tow. But this morning, awakened by that baby's cry; that idyllic picture is crushed by the weight of reality.

There's no more sleeping in on Saturdays, no more time for dumb shows or movies. And given their infinite potential for death and destruction, there is no way I am taking one of my kids to a restaurant other than McDonalds.

As my baby cries in the next room, waiting for me to get up and play, there is a part of me that is actually in a state of grief. With all the years of looking forward to this very day, now that it is here, I have conflicting emotions. I love my baby, and am thankful to God every day for the blessing of a family. Yet at the same time, there is a sense of mourning, a recognition that my old life is over. The decades of doing whatever I want, whenever I want, have suddenly and dramatically shifted. Now the driving force in our family is no longer me, or even my wife, it is this tiny little person who simply wants some love and attention--AT 6:00 AM!!

The Bad News: Your Old Life Is Over

In most of the circles I travel in, there are only a couple of acceptable ways to talk about your children. One way is to update your friends and family about the progress your child is making as they grow. "He can roll over now." "She is sitting up." "He is starting to teethe." "Now she can walk!" The other way to talk is a commentary about what a blessing they are and how being a mom or a dad is the biggest gift on the planet. The only negative comment allowed is one about lack of sleep. And the response we get from our friends and family is some sort of patronizing reflection about how short this season of life is, and to cherish every moment because it goes by so fast.

But these limited options for conversation are not very honest or helpful. While I wholeheartedly agree with all of it--the excitement for growth and development, the incredible blessing of an expanding family, how exhausted I am, or even the reality of how I need to cherish every moment because it will be over before I know it--there is still this hidden part inside of me that I am scared to admit exists.

When I peel back the joy of having a child, the difficulty of the lack of sleep, the pride I have in my wife, underneath I find something dark. It is grief. We've all experienced grief on many different levels. We expect it when a loved one dies, or when we have to move, or we get let go from our job. But are we allowed to feel grief when it comes to having a child? Of course we're not grieving our children, but it *is* this change that's causing the grief.

Part of grief is recognizing that something has changed, and in the case of having a child, *everything* has changed. Some of that change is that our old life is over; it is dead. And if we're going to fully live into this new reality, then we have to do some reflection to make sure we are walking through this transition in a healthy way.

Denial: This is Just Hard Now

The first stage of grief is usually denial. This is my favorite stage; the one where I can cram down all the negative feelings and pretend that everything is going to be OK. There are so many blessings about having a child, so much love and support from family and friends, that it's easy to push down any sense of grief or sadness.

After we had our first baby, there would be many days where people could tell that we were at the end of our rope. Whether we went to a friend's house or headed off to church, we would walk around like zombies, totally strung out from the lack of sleep and the never-ending anxiety of being responsible for this little life. The overwhelming advice was always to *hang in there!*, or that *it will get easier*, or that *this time goes by really fast*. At first I actually believed the advice, and I was prepared for the feeling of grief to be temporary. Soon my son would sleep through the night, have all his teeth, be able to feed himself, be potty trained...

I lived in this stage of denial all the way through the first couple of years of my son's life. It wasn't until we added Baby Number Two that I realized that something was going on inside of me. I could no longer keep a lid on my denial, and all those hidden emotions were starting to manifest themselves in anger. Because my wife was home with the kids and I was able to daily escape to work, this process took longer for me than it did for her. But both of us experienced this transition from denial into anger, though in different times and different ways.

Anger: Is It Even OK To Go There?

Anger is the next step in the grief process. But in the Christian world, is it acceptable to be angry? Was I even allowed to be angry? My wife and I spent 5 years trying to have our son. We wrestled with God and cried with friends. We really wanted a baby of our own. And now that our prayer had become a reality, I was angry? What's up with that?

Because I'm such an upstanding citizen and good Christian I wouldn't really let myself go there. My anger worked its way out in guilt and disappointment. I thought I was a more virtuous and whole person than this. In fact, in the thick of it, I wouldn't have even called it anger, because no one else called it anger, and I didn't want people to think there was something wrong with me.

But upon reflection, there was anger, there had to be. It is impossible to properly grieve your old life without allowing space to be upset somewhere in there. The way I dealt with this was by checking out. Home life was so hard, every minute. I could barely recognize the precious wife of my youth, and all my kids ever did was scream and break things. Being home where I was forced into confronting these dark feelings was not my first choice, so I found myself getting more and more busy at work. I would accept larger projects and take advantage of opportunities to travel. Escape was my coping mechanism, or rather, my avoidance mechanism. Thankfully my wife is more whole than I am, and she had some great friends who walked with her through these moments of anger towards our kids and towards me.

Realizing that escape was not a very good plan, I thought it was time to deal with what was going on inside of me. I did not want to be a distant husband and father. I did not want to live in the past. I had very much wanted to have children, but now that they were here nothing was what I envisioned. This was where the next stage, bargaining, came into play.

Bargaining: Sifting Through All the Pieces

In some areas of grief bargaining can look like trying to make trades or negotiations with God: *If You do this for me then I'll do that...* In the subtle mourning of parenting, this bargaining looks more like actually wrestling with our conflicted emotions and try to whip them into shape. We want to live in the present, to be excited about our kids and our new role. We believe there is no place for anger or avoidance. So we work, we get some help, and we begin to try to put the pieces together.

It was in this stage that my wife and I became frequent buyers at Amazon.com. If there was a problem, then we figured there must be a book out there to help us fix it. We read everything. We read books to help us understand our children's development. We read books to help us figure out their sleep. We read books about how to get them to eat vegetables. We read books about marriage and about how to keep the love alive. We read *everything*. And after reading each book we'd come up with another new game plan, some sort of action strategy that we hoped would solve whatever problem we were facing.

My wife and I worked really hard at trying to understand all the pieces on the table. And once we felt like we had a good idea with what they all were, with the help of these new strategies, we began to attempt to put the picture back together. We instituted date nights, strict bed times, and family dinners. But even with all that work, our past life was more and more a distant memory. And unlike Dorothy, we were losing the hope that we could go back. My wife and I were becoming more and more disconnected, and I felt like I knew even less about parenting than I had when we started!

It is at this point for many parents that depression often shows up. And how we deal with this depression sets the trajectory for the duration of our marriages.

Depression: How Many More Years of This?

Depression is a scary emotion. It is the feeling of being hopeless and helpless. In the grief process it is the point where you have tried everything to no avail. You tried avoiding, fighting and working through it. And at the end of all that work, you find yourself still in the same situation. It's one thing when there was some grief about your old life, but you believed it was fixable or at least temporary--it is completely different to do hard work and realize that nothing has changed.

This feeling of hopelessness is death, especially death in a marriage. Realizing that kids have taken over your life and have become the center of your existence is awful. Being a pastor to children and students, I see countless families who are in a low-level state of depression. Couples don't know how to work through this so they die to their former lives, their former joys, and try to grind it out. But grinding it out is an awful way to live. This grief process is normal and necessary. It's normal to grieve about the old way of life, the carefree life of being childless. But when this grief takes over and seeps to every area of your life, it gets scary. And if you find yourself grieving your marriage, you are in big trouble.

Because of the love we have for our kids, it is natural to grind it out. But that is not the abundant life that God intends for us. In order to walk along the path of everlasting life that God marks out for us, we must continue to put one foot in front of the other and continue walking. Depression halts our footsteps, but healing and hope only happen as we keep putting one foot in front of the other.

If depression is where you find yourself, depressed about this new life, you have to know there is hope. Moving from depression to acceptance is simply an affirmation that, what was, is now over. What will be is still to be determined. You do not have the power to bring back the past, but you can shape the future.

With out being too flip, sometimes the combination of the complete disruption of your old rhythms of life, post-partum chemical and hormonal balances, the added financial burden and other variables seem to be more than we can bear. If this is the case, then simple willpower and prayer may not be able to pull you out of this depression. It has to be OK for you to be honest with how you are really doing and seek help so you can move from depression to acceptance.

Acceptance: This is My Life

If you can own up to the different steps of grief, do the hard work, and keep your feet moving, there truly is light at the end of the tunnel. The final stage in grief is acceptance. Acceptance is not giving up and letting yourself go. Acceptance isn't settling into how hard and difficult life is. That is depression. Acceptance is the simple recognition that the old life is over—but that a new one has appeared in its place.

Once you can get your head around that, you can actually live into this new--and more importantly, abundant--life. You now have the opportunity to live a life *in light* of the reality of little kids, rather than *in spite* of them. It's a life where you once again are in the driver's seat, deciding what you want this life to look like and where you want to go. When we parents live accepting this new reality we are ready and able to live a better and deeper life, one of genuine purpose and joy.

It is a difficult process, one that takes real work. But the effort is so worth it, because at the end you once again have a wide road leading down an amazing adventure. The road may be heading down a different road than you imagined at first, but it is still a road that is ready to be traveled by you and your family. The real question is how are you going to move forward from here? You have been intentional in every area of your life up to this point; going to school, falling in love, getting married, advancing in career, even having a baby. Living into this new family takes just as much intentionality.

A Hidden Grief: Time Alone

The trick is finding the space and time to reflect. It is the loss of this precious alone-time for spiritual growth, exercise, and reflection that is a hidden area of grief and mourning. The same process of grief that we walk through mourning our old life is similar to the one we'll need in grieving our loss of alone-time.

As I've said, it's impossible to live this abundant life without being intentional in our spiritual growth and reflection. To figure out how to have space for this we have to acknowledge that our old rhythms of spiritual growth and reflection will not be a reality here. Let's do some more grieving as we move toward acceptance.

Questions for Reflection:
1) As your old life gets swept away, where have you seen grief creep in?
2) What stage of grief are you in? Or are you having trouble acknowledging your grief in the first place?
3) What stage is or has been the most difficult? Can you see yourself getting to acceptance? How will you begin to move forward?

chapter three: THE DEATH OF QUIET TIME

The Need to Be Alone

It wasn't until I had my kids that I realized that quiet, reading, and reflecting were such an important part of my life. Coming home from work and reading a book or watching TV was the norm. Getting up early to have a devotional time of preparing my heart and mind for the day ahead was the rule, not the exception. Cuddling with my wife as she read her book and I played on my computer was part of the natural rhythm of my time.

As soon as the kids entered the picture, this precious time started disappearing at an alarming rate. When I got home from work, it was obvious that my wife had had a very long and taxing day. In my attempt to be a good husband and father, I took over the kid duty as she made dinner. Gone was coming home and decompressing from work. Heading home was now about ramping up instead of gearing down. Throughout the day, my wife and I would check in with phone calls, pictures, and videos. Sometimes they would be pictures and voicemails of a mom who is so full of joy, and other times they would be calls of desperation and anger. At the first call of the day, you never knew what kind of day it was going to be, but by three in the afternoon, I knew what sort of home I would be heading home to, and I would prepare accordingly.

The plan was to get the kids down by 7:00 p.m. so that we would have some adult time until we went to bed, so we could get up and do it all over again. While that was the plan, add in the natural chaos of nighttime, and it soon became another unmet goal. By the time we got to that adult-time point in the day, the thought of doing something other than watching TV to zone out was a fantasy. We were both fried, and after catching up on the details of the day just finished and the to-do's for the next, we had no more bandwidth for quiet and reflection.

With all the unpredictability of nighttime and compounding sleep depravation, the thought of waking up an hour earlier than I had to felt like an impossibility. Either I was up several times trying to soothe a crying child, or I was awakened by the door crashing open as my daughter came to our bed with all her "stuffies." I know all the books say if we had just let them scream it out, they would have figured it out in a couple of days. But when the choice was needed sleep or teaching our kid a lesson, I always chose sleep. More often than not, I ended up sleeping at the foot of the bed as my son and my daughter invaded our room at different parts of the night. Needless to say, when my alarm went off, I snoozed, in an attempt to prolong the inevitable: another long day of work at my job and my work at home.

The casualty of all this disruption was my inner life. We all need time to think and time to reflect. We all need time to spend with God and be encouraged and fed spiritually. We all need time just to process our days and to develop and assess our plan to live an intentional life.

When that time is gone, we become passive, only reacting to the events in our day, rather then being proactive and determining the course of our days. If we want to do more than just survive, we must find time to be alone.

Love Spending Time With God

I made a covenant with my wife the day we were married. I had settled the issue: this is my wife, and I will be committed to her for my entire life. But this commitment isn't what makes a good marriage. It is the daily connection that re-affirms this commitment and keeps it an act of love rather than simply an act of will.

I have a similar goal and rhythm to my devotional life as in my marriage. My devotions have been the time when I re-connect my heart to the faith and convictions I have settled on in my head. Without quiet time in my walk with God, my fuse gets short and my view gets narrow. When I am connected to God I see evidence of His new life in me: love, joy, peace, patience, kindness, goodness, faithfulness, gentleness, and self-control. Without my regular time of devotions, I would simply have had an intellectual assent to my faith, but no heart connection, where a vibrant relationship with God could actually mold and shape, heal and transform, making me more and more into His image.

In the B.C. (Before Children) past, my alone-time began in the mornings with a quiet time. I would wake up, get a cup of coffee and sit at our kitchen table, ready to get my head and heart right for the day ahead. This time has looked different through the many different seasons of my life. For a large chunk of my adulthood, this connection time was a regular part of my life, a specific time set aside for prayer, study and reflection. It was one of the most important parts of my daily routine.

I Need Some 'Me' Time

Not only do I need quiet time to make space for God to move in my life, but I also just need time to be quiet. There are so many things competing for my thoughts and attention. I have added responsibilities at my job, I have friends that I am losing connection with, a wife who needs help and support, and young children who I long to build heart-strands with. But all this output leaves me exhausted and empty.

Even the most extroverted person in the world cannot cope with all the demands little kids put on our lives. Because exhaustion has settled in, whenever there is even a moment of quiet, the last thing I want to do is think about anything. At this point I will watch anything on TV just to give my mind a break. Yet an unreflective life only keeps the real issues, concerns, hopes, and fears unrealized. Socrates even acknowledged this when he said that, "An unexamined life is not worth living." These pent-up emotions can cause trouble because they are often let out at moments of weakness, and communicated in hurtful ways.

Throughout the course of raising babies, toddlers and little kids, I have tried just about everything under the sun to get this alone-time. I'll tell you what doesn't work: arriving home from work to a frazzled wife and a chaotic house, declaring that I need some alone-time, and then heading off to the gym.

See, my wife is in just as dire need of alone time as I am. The more we can communicate our needs, the more we can accommodate each other. We have a much better marriage and are much better parents when she gives me space to go for a run and I give her space to take a nap, grab a coffee with a friend, and get her nails done. The tyranny of the urgent will make this appear impossible, but our long-term emotional health demands that we have to figure it out and make it work.

Grace For This Season

The truth is that there is no way you will ever be alone like you were in the past. As I tried every day to wake up early and spend some time with God like I did in the past, only to fail day after day, guilt began to take over. So, now on top of not having any time for prayer or reflection or exercise, I got to add guilt to the list of negative emotions I was trying to manage.

As a pastor, this guilt that is piled on as I struggle to spend time with God is even heavier. It's my job, for crying out loud, to be connected to God, to be growing in my faith, and to be intentional in my spiritual development. But kids are the great equalizer. They bring all of us to our knees as we realize that there is no way we can spend the kind of time with God that we did before they were born. What if, during this unique time, of sleepless nights and total invasion of personal space, we might actually be in the exact right place to learn a brand new spiritual lesson: We cannot do it on our own.

We are saved by grace. There is nothing we can do to earn God's favor. And for whatever reason, we seem to arrive at this place where we are mostly put together and somehow think it is our effort that got us there, and our effort that continues to earn us favor with God. But just like our kids, who are helpless without us, who are self-absorbed, and who give very little back compared to what they take, we might once again settle into this worldview in our walk with God.

We are in a season where we have very little to give spiritually. We cannot wake up earlier, we cannot come home later, and there is no way that at the end of our day we will bust open our Bibles and start to pray. That is a recipe for instant sleep. But the wonderful truth is, God isn't upset with us. He created us and He knows exactly what is going on inside of us.

There is no condemnation for those who are in Christ. We are loved and forgiven. We are God's dearly-loved children. And in this season where His children are working their tails off trying to figure out this parenting thing, we will only find mercy and grace from God.

The Grieving Process

There is no way we will be able to move forward until we first get rid of our guilt, because guilt over grieving is stalling our progress. Once we get over it, we can continue on in the process of working through the grief over the long-gone rhythms of our old life and our old experience of quiet time. They may come back some day, but that day is on the distant horizon. The only way forward is through grieving the old ways. It is only by walking through the denial, anger, bargaining, and depression will we be ever be able to get to a place of acceptance.

This place of acceptance in our devotional life does not mean giving up and putting our faith on hold until our kids grow up and move out. If that's your mentality, you are actually still in the land of depression and hopelessness. The land we want to live in is the land where we have a growing faith and have time for reflection in light of our current realities, not in spite of them.

This is Not a New Problem

For all of human history people have worked crazy hours and have raised children. For thousands of years people of faith have been doing these things too. We are part of a long line of hard workers, who love God and have wanted to raise their children to love God. In order to do that well, we can't live in the past with our past rhythms; we must develop new rhythms that will work in the new realities of our life.

An hour in the morning before the world wakes up and an hour at the gym before I come home from work might have to be put on hold for now. To attempt these and fail to do them only to feel guilt isn't a way forward, either. To attempt them at the expense of my wife and children isn't a way forward. Not attempting at all isn't an option. Acceptance is recognizing that this is a brand new world. So, what will this new world look like?

What Will This New World Look Like?

This is the question that must be answered if we are going to take our faith seriously. We will not survive over the long haul without space for God to refine us and shape us. We are broken people in need of repair. And when we are at our wits end, when our brokenness comes out in the worst ways, we are in the greatest need. There is no option to shelve our faith for the next two years, which means the next five, or forever.

In the core of our being we want to be all that God has designed us to be, to have an abundant life, with a healthy and passionate marriage, with children who love God and will follow Him all of their days. This is a noble calling, and not for the faint at heart. It is a calling that takes strength and hard work. It is hard work to figure out our issues, to grieve properly, and to be intentional in this new world we live in. Parenting is not an easy task and a difficult calling. There is no room for slacking. Your family name, the health of your marriage, and the passing on of faith to the next generation are at stake. We need to figure out our issues and then get to the place where we can accept this new world, and begin to thrive in it, not just survive.

Questions for Reflection:
1) B.C. (Before Children), where did you go to be quiet, reflect, and recharge?
2) What are ways that you and your spouse can give each other this needed time?
3) If you are not going to put your faith on hold, what does a spiritual life in during this unique time of life look like for you?

chapter four: THE STAKES COULD NOT BE HIGHER

Say No to Boz

When my son was around two years old, my wife brought home a DVD of a cartoon that was supposed to help him develop his faith and understanding of Biblical concepts. Because I was all for trying to find ways for my boy to love God, and TV was what captured his attention the most, I saw no downside. That was, until I actually turned the video on.

To my horror, a green bear named Boz, with a high-pitched voice, showed up on the screen, singing and playing with kids. I started to have Barney flashbacks, and I think I even threw up a little in my mouth. It took everything in me to suffer through a 22-minute episode about "The Love of God". My son was hooked. I was horrified.

Thankfully, my wife is a more mature person than I am. Her reasoning was sound, and her argument was compelling, but my immaturity was immense. It took longer than you might expect, but she eventually talked me down off the cliff. This was the basic discussion:

Me: "This cartoon is a total joke, and makes our faith in God simple and trite. With all that God has done in our life, there is no way we are going to hand our son a bowl full of Christian cheese. It will wreck him." (I thought that was a pretty convincing argument.)

My wife: "Hey Ben, this show was not made for you. It is simple and trite because it was written for our son, WHO IS TWO YEARS OLD!"

It was at this point I realized that the task of passing on a vibrant faith in a God who is alive was going to be much more difficult than I thought. I didn't even have my head around the basic tasks of parenting, let alone the weight of helping them love God.

It's one thing to be a slacker struggling with my own faith, my own identity, and my own marriage. These are emotions that were normal for me and in many ways I enjoyed the wrestling. I found life in striving to know God in a real and vibrant way through peaks and valleys. But now, I had this added anxiety of being responsible for not only the emotional and physical development of my boy, but his spiritual development as well.

Because I had grown accustomed to being spent and running on empty, I was consumed with the tyranny of the urgent and therefore found zero space to be intentional about the important things. Piled on top of this was the fact that I still carried some residual grief from the death of my former way of life. Fantasy became my only escape; the fantasy of a time when I would have everything figured out and life would be easier; a time when I would have the maturity and emotional space to actually parent in a way that cares for all the needs of my kids. I fantasized about a time when it would all work out and be easier. Because this was my secret fantasy, I can smell it a mile away in my friends.

A Typical Approach

We have some dear friends who are just a couple of years behind us in marriage and kids. Having babies was an awful transition for this couple. But you would have to read between the lines to see what I am talking about. You see, they are a good Christian family who love God and strive to have their kids love God, too. They are involved in a great church, a good small group, and a couple of solid play groups. But if you listened closely, you would see this fantasy rising up. It was subtle and makes sense, but the sum total of the evidence was alarming.

The fantasy is simple, and dangerous.

"I am so glad to be pregnant and start our family, but I can't wait to finally have this baby."

"Isn't my baby so beautiful? Once she is sleeping through the night, it will be so great."

"It is getting so hard to carry this baby everywhere. Once she can walk, we will be able to do so much more."

"This potty training thing is harder than we thought."

"Once they can (dress themselves, go to preschool, start kindergarten, be in school all day, graduate high school, move out)... Then life will be better."

What an awful habit to get into: to always think that at some point things will get better and therefore easier.

After doing student ministry for over 15 years, I can tell you beyond the shadow of a doubt that parenting never gets easier. The stakes only get higher, and the effort needed only increases. When we fantasize about a time when we will have our lives back for ourselves, we end up actually doing very little. We find ourselves waiting for a magical time when it will become apparent that our kids are ready to receive all that we have teach them. And we think, "When that happens, we will actually start parenting in an intentional way." But that is a fantasy; that time will never happen.

In some sense, we expect that our kids will eventually figure it out. When we were potty-training our son, my wife kept telling me to relax. He wasn't going to go to kindergarten in diapers; he would figure it out. Sure enough, he did. The same philosophy didn't work with vegetables. We didn't want to fight nightly about veggies, so I figured he would grow into them at some point. Five years later, vegetables are not happening. I thought that eating cereal with his fingers was just what little babies did and he would at some point be a big boy and start to use a spoon. Nope.

Even though our good friends are at the very beginning of this parenting journey, the trajectory is clear, at least to me. My time in student ministry is piled high with stories of parents who keep waiting for that perfect time to start being intentional in the faith development of their kids. If you think about it, it does seem to make sense that there is a certain time that is more beneficial than another to help your child develop their faith.

After all, what kind of faith can a newborn have? What could a baby who can just crawl around really understand about God? What Bible story is even appropriate for a toddler? Is kindergarten the time to answer the questions about life and death? Won't it freak out my elementary-aged child to talk about Jesus' death on a cross? Middle-schoolers don't even think abstractly yet (some people would argue whether they think at all!) How in the world do they develop an actual relationship with God?

The answer is, there is *no* time that is perfect. In fact, our relational development and our faith development never occur due to one intentional conversation or activity. There is no such thing as quality time. Raising a toddler is all about *quantity* time. During all the time we have together, we add little bits of sand and dirt to the concrete mixture. Little by little these conversations, experiences, and activities build the foundation for kids' love and trust in you--and in God.

So, if we wait for that perfect, *quality*, time to begin these conversations, we will realize that all we have done is punted the spiritual development of our kids so far down the field that any sort of conversation would seem forced, out of place. The truth is, being intentional with our child's faith development begins right now. It doesn't matter if they are three months or eleven years old. It is always awkward to broach the subject. You see, faith development is not like potty-training. It doesn't happen in its own, "natural" time, it only happens when we intentionally and regularly pick up our faith and our kids and consistently bring them to Jesus, until they can do it on their own.

This intentional process is illustrated by one of the more famous stories in scripture.

A Unique Approach

In Luke chapter 5 we find a story of faith that is unique, yet seems to parallel the task of parenting quite closely. Early in His ministry, Jesus had been teaching from the scriptures with a unique authority that resonated with the people. We all have deep-seated questions about the things of God, and we long for someone to lay it down in a clear and authoritative way. This very common need was satisfied completely in the person of Jesus.

Along with His charisma and authority, Jesus demonstrated power in the physical and spiritual realms. He cast out demons, healed the sick, and gave sight to the blind. The combination of His teaching and power became legendary and soon, wherever Jesus was, a large crowd was there as well.

It was in this context that four people with extraordinary faith decided to be intentional about bringing hope and salvation to their friend. These four picked up the mat of their paralyzed friend and carried him to the house where Jesus was teaching. Arriving at the home, they noticed there was no way for them to get close to Jesus because of the crowd. This small obstacle didn't trouble these determined friends. They simply took matters into their own hands. Without delay they climbed to the top of the house with their paralytic friend in tow, tore open the roof and put him in the path of Jesus. And it was at this point that Jesus affirmed the men's faith and saved their friend.

I don't think it's too much of a stretch for us as parents to realize that our little baby boy or baby girl is helpless and lost. There is no possible way for them to come to Jesus all by themselves. Part of the parenting task is to grab hold of the mat and overcome whatever obstacles might come for the single-minded purpose of placing our child before the feet of Jesus.

We may not have crowds or the destruction of property to overcome, but our obstacles are just as daunting. We have our own faith we need to wrestle with and come to terms with. We are inexperienced and lost as parents. Faith is a mystery, and we have insecurities combined with exhaustion that weigh on us to the point of paralysis. But if we wimp out and give up, there will be no one else to come after us and pick up our child's mat. This daunting responsibility is ours, and ours alone.

It is an act of faith, this task of intentionally bringing our kids to Jesus, this intentional development of their faith. The truth is, there is no magic pill or system that guarantees success. While our intentionality may not guarantee our child's own faith someday, doing nothing and being passive almost closes the door on this possibility. This is probably why it's called faith.

As parents who long for our children to love God someday, we must get past our own junk, our own issues and baggage. We are finished with the part of our life that was all about our personal odyssey and us. For this season is about living into today, into this moment, and mustering up every ounce of faith that we have so we can pick up a corner of the mat and drag our child to the feet of Jesus. We cannot wait for our kids to grow up, to learn to read, to ask the right questions, to understand for themselves how silly Boz is. Today is all we have; today is the day. We must jump in and go for it, because our faith, and our actions are what ultimately contribute to the development, or atrophy of the faith of our children.

But before we jump into the how-to's--stay with me now--we must wrestle with one more thing. We must get our head around the proper expectations to bring with us when we attempt to be intentional about the faith development of our children. In fact, when we kill our unrealistic expectations, we can stop being scared that we are doing it wrong or what the outcome will or won't be. It is through realistic expectations that we are free to engage to help nurture our children's faith out of our love for Jesus and not out fear.

Questions for Reflections:
1) Are there ways that you are already putting your faith issues on your children?
2) When is that magical time you keep telling yourself when things will be finally better?
3) What are ways that you can begin to carry the mat toward Jesus for your child?

chapter five: WHAT NEEDS TO CHANGE?
(MY KIDS, MY EXPECTATIONS, ME?)

Be Careful What You Read

When I was in college I read a book that rocked my world more than any other up to that time. I was just starting to really grow in my walk with God and my bible study leader handed me an old, worn out book called, "Power and Purpose in Prayer." Written by E.M. Bounds around the turn of the century, this book had no pictures or graphics to catch my attention. But what was written inside was rich, deep, and earth-shattering. In fact, I'm not yet recovered from it!

It has been more than 15 years since I read this book, but I am still haunted by the picture presented of what the prayer life of a godly man and Christian leader should be. I read story after story of Puritan men who would wake up in the 4's, retire to a special prayer closet and spend hours praying and seeking God. To bring home the point, Bounds paints a picture of floorboards sanded and grooved by those faithful knees.

As an idealistic young man, this book became my benchmark of Christian discipleship and formation. The problem was that I was nineteen, in college, and loved sleep. My theme verse in college, and even today, is

Lamentations 3:23 "Great is His faithfulness; His mercies begin afresh each morning." I have always wrestled with the big ideas of who I am, can be, and should be. And to make things worse, I have never been able to live into *any* of those expectations.

That Lamentations verse was always my theme, every morning, every first of the month, or every beginning of a new semester and year. You see, I began the start of the day, month, whatever, painting a picture of who I thought God was calling me to be. In college, because of this verse, it meant that I would faithfully set my alarm for 5:00 am to spend my time with God. Monday the alarm would go off, and I was good to go, tired but expectant. I would roll out of bed and do my faithful duty. Tuesday would be harder, and Wednesday was a no-go. I would spend the rest of the week feeling guilty for failing and waiting for the next Monday to live fully into Lamentations.

The Never-Ending Unrealistic Expectations

As I reflect, I realize that this pattern of life still plagues me. I still set my alarm for 5:00 am, with hopes to have the prayer life of a 19th century Puritan farmer. Why? I have no idea; except that some book I read told me I should. I live with this low-grade anxiety and guilt that I am failing. This anxiety has haunted not just my prayer life, but also every area of my life.

When I was dating my wife, I read a book about what a good marriage should look like. Since then, I've heard speakers talk about the need for maturity, leadership, and romance as my role in marriage, only to find myself failing all the time. I know it is my job to initiate prayer in my marriage, but I suck at it, and don't do it. And sure enough every new week, month, year, I lean into the new mercies of God and paint a new picture to live into. Without fail, I end up failing, then waiting for the next beginning to try again.

Having kids only magnified my expectations and highlighted my ineptness. Books, seminars, friends, are all reinforcing a common picture of parenting--parenting that is full of grace, intention, and spiritual depth. I was all excited to have kids, to pass on our family traditions and our faith to our little children. This was so exciting and encouraging until I actually tried to pull it off with my actual children, which was certainly not at all like the idealized version in my head. Mealtime, bedtime, car rides, all of it--have proven to not be the hoped-for sacred times, but continual reminders that I am woefully inept at my calling as a dad. Oh, how I need to live into the truth of God's mercies to be new every morning.

Now, throw in my job and other relationships, and quickly I've realized there is no way I can possibly live up to all of the expectations I've claimed for myself. To have the prayer life, spiritual depth and knowledge I want is a full-time job. To have a marriage that is passionate and romantic takes parts of me that are woefully underdeveloped. To be the pastor or professional I desire to be, with all the expanding opportunities, seems to only conflict with my other passions and desires. Throw in kids, and I am sunk.

While I am running around attempting to manage every obligation-- job, family, friend--I discover my fuse is getting shorter and shorter. Now, in the precious time I have to be around my children, I notice I have nothing left to give, and I just want it to be bedtime. Our children are gigantic sponges who soak up everything we say and do, seen and seemingly unseen. Instead of being full of intention, it becomes the time where we are the most overwhelmed and spent. Our kids need the best of us, but how do we give it to them when every other area of our lives is demanding just as much of our best time and attention?

There Has Got To Be A Better Way

To pull off the perfect version of "Christian/Pastor/Husband/Father/Friend/Writer/Runner" I would need less than four hours of sleep. Every night. As I mentioned earlier, I love sleep. So I've found my choice is to either be exhausted, trying to do too much and have all my relationships suffer, or sleep more and feel guilty for being such a slacker, longing for the next Monday when I can experience God's mercy anew. There is no way this can be what Jesus was talking about when He said that His yoke is easy and His burden light, can it?

As I've been trying to figure this out, I've come to an interesting conclusion. People have been having babies since the dawn of time, and have been following God and passing their faith on to the next generation for just as long. Ever since God told Moses in Deuteronomy 6:4-8 that parents are supposed to impress their faith upon their children, to talk about them at home and when you walk on the road, parents have been compelled to pass on the story of faith to their children. And since this faith has successfully been passed on for the last 3500 years, maybe, I thought, I'm making this a little harder than it needs to be.

I think part of the problem is that we have developed a false view of time. We actually have more free time than any generation in all of history, and yet at the exact same time, have the absolute *least.*

All of our ancestors had to work all day, every day, just to survive; work from sunrise to sundown, collecting water and fire wood, working the field and working in the factory. This work was not so they could take a vacation to Disneyland, this was work so they could have enough food to make it another day. After a long day of all this work, it was off to bed to get some rest, so they could do it all again the next day. Those in the Judeo-Christian tradition would take one day off to rest, to Sabbath: to take time to re-connect with God and with their families. Yet even with this full work schedule, our ancestors managed to raise kids who become productive members of society, and many of them successfully passed down their faith from one generation to the next. Was there some sort of trick they knew about that we are missing? I don't think so. But I do think they looked at life and work differently.

Part of the problem is we no longer work to survive, but instead work to maintain a certain lifestyle. And this lifestyle has become all-consuming, leaving very little margin for rest and connection. There is no place for Sabbath in our context. A day off is simply a day packed full of everything you couldn't get to in the workweek: errands, yard work, sports, travel, and often, even more workweek work.

This kind of lifestyle leaves little room for addressing the sort of anxieties that fill our minds as parents of young children. Are they developing correctly? When will they walk? Is their speech delayed? What preschool will they attend? Which dance class should they take? How much TV should they watch? If you think about it, we actually have so much free time that miscellaneous activities and anxieties fill our life and minds.

And the worst part of all is these anxieties get wrapped up into the unrealistic expectations surrounding personal development, comparing performance and competence to our peers, and unrealistic fears surrounding our children's safety. It might be helpful to turn off the TV, disconnect the internet, and put the phone away, at least for a minute. Then take a deep breath, grab a cup of coffee, and rest.

We Simply Must Uncover What Is Already There

In this place of rest we actually have time to reflect and examine our lives and our expectations. It's in this place of rest we realize how much time and energy we pour into things that have little value, completely disregarding the things of greatest value. In order to settle in and celebrate all that God has for us while we are raising little kids, we might need to reexamine our personal expectations, our lifestyle choices, and the mental tapes we play over and over in our head.

Raising children is not rocket science, but there is a science to it. Raising children in a way that nurtures our own faith while passing it on is actually part of our DNA. It is how we were created to be. It has been placed in the innermost fibers of our being. In fact, there is nothing new in the pages ahead except for an uncovering of what already is.

It is in our hearts to walk closely with God. The author of Ecclesiastes affirms we were created with eternity in our hearts. Our kids get this, and at one point in our lives we did too. As adults we've become "self-sufficient" and, in the process, reduced God to an absent Grandpa in the sky loving us from afar and providing some special treats along the way. Yet, if we rest, we reawaken to the truth that there is a very alive God who desires to transform us and empower us to live a full and abundant life. It is in our hearts to do this. It is simply a matter of creating space to experience it.

It is also in our hearts to be totally connected to our spouse. Remember your wedding day, standing in front of all your friends and family? I do. I was so hopeful for the life ahead. It was very easy to say the vows presented by the pastor. Sickness and health, rich and poor... But as the years go on, and the road of life takes some treacherous turns, the honeymoon turns to dry commitment, and sometimes even worse. All of the pits and valleys of life are a part of every life. We have the choice to walk alone through them, or to rely on our spouse and friend and walk through them together. Two is always better than one. It is in our hearts to be this. It is simply a matter of remembering the love of our youth.

It is in our hearts to have our kids know they are deeply loved by us and by the God who created them. Isn't it strange that we long for our kids to feel this way about us and about God, yet often manage to have them experience the exact opposite? We work hard to provide them *things*, yet what they need most is our time, not more things. We are so fried from maintaining our lifestyle that we have little emotional space, so we kid ourselves into thinking that buying presents replaces our presence. This rat race depletes us emotionally, physically and spiritually, and instead of passing on love and grace from us and God, we model a God who is distant and unconnected to their lives, because He is unconnected to ours. While this may be the situation today, it is in our hearts for our kids to know our deep love for them and their heavenly Father's as well. It is simply a matter of us modeling the true heart of God for our children.

To make these longings of our hearts a reality, we must step back, rest, Sabbath. It is only in this Sabbath space that we can begin to get head and heart around what God has already put in our hearts, and then live into that reality. In order to pull this off we need to stop pretending we have it all together, reshape our expectations of spiritual formation both for us and our children, and join in community with people who will help us live it out.

Spiritual discipline is not about us working harder. It is about us responding with an open heart to invitation to walk even closer with our Creator, Redeemer, and Sustainer.

Once we have begun to come to terms with some of our own issues, maybe we can begin to find freedom in expressing our guilt, disappointment, and frustrations along with our joys, successes, and surprises. We need this sort of candor if we are going to allow space for God to reshape our expectations of following Him during this season.

Let's take a look together at what it might look like to re-examine our lives from a bit of a different perspective to see all the places that God is already at work, and longs to be even more intimately involved.

Questions for Reflection:
1) List out your personal, family, and spiritual expectations. How realistic are they?
2) If your children were reflective, what do you think they would say are the things most important to you? In other words—what are you modeling about your priorities?
3) What could change so that they would see—and say-- your faith and your family are what is most important to you?

section two:

RAISING LITTLE CHILDREN AS A SPIRITUAL DISCIPLINE

chapter one: THE MINISTRY OF PRESENCE: AN INTRODUCTION

Gearing Up For The Marathon

Over the last few years I've gotten into long distance running. Because I am a larger person, I realized that speed running was never going to be my thing. But because I am a prideful man, I needed some reason to run, something to compete against, a bar to strive for. Since most people run for speed, I saw an opening in the long-run category. Something I love about running long distances is nobody asks how long it takes or how fast I run. They're simply impressed that I went out and ran 10 miles that day. This subtle difference in focus proved to be just enough to satisfy my ego and help me stay in shape.

Surprisingly, running long distances has changed the way in which I view food. Until recently, food was something I would consume for any reason. If it was mealtime, I was ready. If I was bored: snack time. If I was stressed, depressed, anxious, or even excited, it was time to eat. Because I ate so frequently I never really thought about food or its role in my life.

Once I started running long distances, I realized that I needed to eat differently. If I enjoyed a large burrito for lunch and went for a long run that afternoon, I was destined for an embarrassing experience behind a bush. But if I ate a balanced meal full of carbohydrates and protein the night before, I was full of energy for my run. As I ran longer and longer distances, I also learned that I had to eat along the way.

When I was a non-runner this was the strangest thought: to bring a camel-pack with food and water to eat while I run. But after you've run for three hours, you have completely depleted any and all nutrition that was once stored in your body. It is amazing the difference a bite of a power bar makes after running for an hour with a couple more hours to go. And what a disaster occurs when I think I can pull off the run without the right amount of food or water.

For the longest time I heard that life, faith, and parenting are all akin to a marathon. Once I got my first marathon under my belt I began to have a better understanding of how intentional we must be in these areas if we are going to finish the race at all, let alone finish well. This picture began to make more and more sense as I reflected on my life and my faith and realized that I was worn out, depleted, and had little to no ability to muster up the strength to continue well on this journey.

Prayer Is Not The Meal

In the marathon of faith and parenting, one of the main pictures I had in my mind about prayer is as a meal. After all, in order to live my life the way God desires me to live, I must have energy to make it through my day. When I pray, I am refilled, re-oriented and ready to accomplish all that God has for me. My early diagnosis was that I wasn't eating well enough for this marathon of parenting. I had been sleep-deprived and every routine that used to bring me life had come to a screeching halt. I used to have all the space in the world to recharge and eat spiritually. I used to read books, journal, pray, memorize scripture, and do it consistently.

Once kids entered the scene, the space for these activities seemed to disappear. My solution was to wake up earlier, stay up later to squeeze in some prayer time so I would have the spiritual energy and awareness to run this race well. My exhaustion, I thought, must be about not getting enough fuel. I needed to eat more. But the more I wrestled with my faith, with myself, and with God I came to a different conclusion. Prayer is *not* a meal.

My prayer life--my connection to the living God--is really nothing like having a meal. If it were, then it would make sense that my spiritual stomach is continually in need of refilling, like a battery continually in need of recharging. But meals for energy, or charging up batteries, assumes that there are isolated times in our day where I connect with God, get juiced up, and then go out with this power and live the life God calls me to live.

This picture misses the true invitation that God has for us. God's desire is that we are not only in relationship with Him, but continually *connected* to Him. The relationship that we are invited into is more like a lamp that is plugged into the wall. A lamp that is running on batteries has a limited life expectancy because at some point those batteries will fail. But a lamp that is connected to the socket on the wall will give light forever, because what it is directly connected to is the source of power, not a small storage of power. If the lamp is not plugged in, then there is no light.

This may sound overwhelming, being connected to God all the time. If I can barely find time to be connected to God once a day to charge me up for a couple of hours, how in the world will I find the time and space to be connected to God all day, every day? When Paul says to pray continually in 1 Thessalonians 5:17 this is supposed to be an invitation to a new way to relate with God. It is not meant to crush our spirits or to be another benchmark that we fail to meet.

This concept of connection is meant as an invitation rather than a challenge. Maybe instead of a lamp connected to the wall as the main mental picture of this prayer life, there might be one that is more helpful. The word Spirit, in both Greek and Hebrew means *breath*. God breathed life into Adam, and when we become Christians we become born anew through the Spirit, and are indwelled by the Spirit. Now God is just as close as our very breath.

Most of us are totally unaware of the fact that we are breathing. We know we breathe, but we are so used to it that it's just something we do. As I've learned how to run long, I've also learned how to breathe. Being aware of my breathing allows me to stay focused and keep my body under control.

What if this invitation that God has for us is not one more thing that we are to add onto our plate, but simply an invitation to become aware of something we're already doing, to become *aware* of our spiritual breathing? God is obviously in love with us, involved with us and with our families. These are truths that are expressed all throughout scripture. The invitation is for us to re-open our eyes, to see, and live into, the places where God is already at work, and celebrate this reality.

This view of prayer is actually not new or revolutionary. Another book I read when I was in college and re-read a couple of years ago is from a simple monk who had a unique approach to the way he worked out his walk with God. Brother Lawrence was a lay monk who lived in France in the 1600's, and the book is a record of conversations he had with a fellow monk, along with a collection of some of his letters. And the result, a simple and short book called, *Practicing the Presence of God*, completely changed how I understand prayer—and how I understand parenting.

Practicing the Presence of God

In every spiritual discipline book I have ever read, somewhere near the front is a quotation from 1 Timothy 4:7 "Train yourself for godliness." Training involves time and effort. And as we strive to be more godly, we are expected to build spiritual disciplines into our lives; disciplines such as Solitude, Memorization, Study, Prayer, Fasting, Giving, etc. While these things are great and important, what I have found, as a parent of a young child, is that I am defeated before I even head off to the spiritual gym. I am so exhausted from life and have absolutely zero space for anything other than the effort to keep the household running. The thought of adding another discipline to the mix when I can rarely get up before the kids and spend even a few minutes in quiet reflection and prayer is depressing and discouraging.

Brother Lawrence offers the weary parent a way forward, an invitation to a deeper, fuller walk with God, even in the midst of the chaos of parenting. What made Brother Lawrence so unique is that he pushed back against the conventional wisdom of his time and of his peers. Back then and, I think, still today, prayer, and all spiritual disciplines, were seen as additions to our lives, strengthening and refining our faith so we could live into the fullest person God has for us to be. But for Brother Lawrence, his "quiet times" seemed awkward and forced. How could he regulate his devotion to God? Instead, he walked with God in such a way that his entire life was a "continual exercise of love, and doing all things for His sake." It didn't matter if he was participating in appointed time for prayer, washing dishes, or running errands, every single thing he did all day long was done with the recognition that he was connected to God, and chose to have every aspect of his life be a reflection of the love of God.

Brother Lawrence commented that most people get stalled out in their walks with God because their devotional life was solely wrapped up in penances. This sort of prayer life denies the love of God and grace offered to us in Jesus Christ. Brother Lawrence fully embraced this love and grace, and chose to live a life in response. I love the way he reflected on his days:

"He examined himself how he had discharged his duty; if he found well, he returned thanks to God; if otherwise, he asked pardon; and without being discouraged, he set his mind right again, and continued his exercise of the presence of God, as if he had never deviated from it."

For Brother Lawrence, practicing the presence of God was simply becoming aware again of his breath. Not just the inhaling of oxygen, but of the very presence of the Holy Spirit in all the sacred and common things that fill every day. And in every action of every day he attempted lived in a way that reflected the love of God.

Raising a Toddler as a Spiritual Discipline

Instead of taking on another task, carving out another hour in the day for a discipline that will lead towards godliness, maybe God is inviting you to re-examine this chaotic and messy season you find yourself in. Spiritual disciplines are designed to strengthen our connection with God, heighten our senses to His leadings, and build our spiritual muscles. During this time where there is limited time and space for traditional quiet times, maybe this is the exact right time to rediscover a spiritual discipline that doesn't seem to get a lot of airplay. It is the one practiced by Brother Lawrence in a little monastery in France over 400 years ago.

Practicing the presence of God is reminding ourselves that we are spiritually breathing. More than oxygen for our lungs, we are connected to God through the breath of the Holy Spirit. And every moment of every day is an invitation not only to worship God and celebrate His love and grace, but to also partner with Him in His purposes.

Your primary God-given responsibility during this small window of time is to care for your small child. And while this sounds romantic and beautiful on paper, we all know that the way it gets lived out is loud and messy. Maybe God desires for us to not just recharge our batteries so we can have the patience to make it through the day without losing our cool; maybe God is already involved and present in our homes and in the lives of our children. Maybe God is fully present in the mess and volume that seems to define your home. And maybe God's desire for you in this season of life is for you to recognize these places, partner with Him, and be a vehicle to fully express the love of God toward your spouse and towards your children.

Practicing the presence of God is the simplest of all disciplines, yet seems to be the most difficult to accomplish. The day in the life of a toddler is the exact opposite of quiet and solitude, my two personal favorite disciplines. But since quiet and solitude need to be put on hold for a while, my desire for myself and my prayer for you is that we would embrace the chaos, embrace the ruined furniture, embrace the screaming and crying, and become aware of the presence of God so we can experience and reflect God's love and grace.

Breathe in, breathe out.

Breathe in, breathe out.

Questions for Reflection:
1) What are some of the spiritual disciplines you have tried? Which ones have been beneficial and which ones have you struggled with?
2) Do you think of your prayer life more as eating meals or recharging, or as breathing?
3) How do these different pictures impact your view of prayer and its importance?
4) Does practicing the presence of God sound more like an invitation or a challenge? Why?

chapter two: BREAKFAST: THE MOST IMPORTANT MEAL OF THE DAY

5:30 AM--Really?

There is something strange going on. You are awake, yet every indicator says the opposite should be true. It is dark outside, your spouse is still sleeping, and your body is wrecked. The clock is not even in the sixes. You ask yourself, "What is going on? Why am I awake?" There are usually only a couple of possible reasons for this.

Usually the culprit is a screaming child in the next room, ready to get out of the crib and begin the day. Sometimes the screaming happens in the middle of the night, and you've given in and let them sleep with you. This was a great plan, at least until they begin to rustle and stick their toes up your nose. Or, as they get a little older, more and more it is the pitter-patter of little feet leaving the comfort and safety of their bed to explore the living room, kitchen, and finally your room. No matter the variation on the theme, the reality is the same: your child is up, so now you are up, and there is no chance to get back to bed.

It may only be 5:30 in the morning, but this day is in full swing, and the trajectory of the day is being set with or without you. Being exhausted often alters our thinking and judgment, but this morning we decide to take control of our tired body and consider a new way to approach the morning together. Before we can fully live into the fullness of this brand new day, we must first drag ourselves out of bed, give our little guy a hug and kiss, and stumble to turn on the coffee. In a matter of minutes we will have that warm cup of coffee to our lips and the much-needed caffeine rushing through our veins. Let's take a minute of silence in gratitude for the modern coffeemaker!

Now, at 5:45, it's time to jump into another full day. The best part about this day is that it hasn't even started yet. Nothing has gone wrong, the kids are fully rested, and they are ready to go. Their only desire is to interact with us and get some food in their bellies. Talk about a low bar for success! So, no matter what yesterday looked like, with its successes and failures, today is brand-new, and just like every morning, God's mercies are brand-new once again. There is no need to start from a point of deficit or guilt, we start from a place of grace. This is a brand new day, and it is GAME ON!

Breakfast Really is the Most Important Meal of the Day

Common wisdom tells us that breakfast is the most important meal of the day. According to webmd.com, "While adults need to eat breakfast each day to perform their best, kids need it even more. Their growing bodies and developing brains rely heavily on the regular intake of food. When kids skip breakfast, they can end up going for as long as eighteen hours without food, and this period of semi-starvation can create a lot of physical, intellectual, and behavioral problems for them." (http://www.webmd.com/diet/guide/most-important-meal)

While it may not seem like it right now, our child's body is depleted and in desperate need for nourishment. The biggest win in this moment is to keep the good feelings rolling. They don't really know that they are hungry, but they are, and the sooner we can get some good, quality food in their bellies, the better our chances of maintaining peace, love and affection in the day. But breakfast isn't just about getting the right nutrients in their body. Breakfast is the official start of the day and the way it proceeds communicates a ton about you, your values, and the intention in which you pour into your child.

Breakfast is just as important for souls as for bodies. While food is important nourishment for our bodies, meals together are important nourishment to our souls. I know that the last thing in the world you really want to do is begin making an elaborate breakfast at 6:00 in the morning. I mean, it is still dark outside, for crying out loud. But creating a sacred space and time in the morning, every morning is so valuable.

Because of everyone's hectic work schedule and commitments, we found that breakfast is really the only regular time in the day that our entire family is at home together. Right now, sleeping in until the last possible minute until you hop in the shower, get ready, and head out the door, might not be the best call. This is the time when we can actually sit down together, see each other, and share life.

Let's be honest. "Sharing life" is kind of a joke when your child is a toddler. It is often a moment of intention and beauty, worthy of a Christmas card, only to be ruined by flying food and spilled milk. Of course this exact moment isn't amazing and won't be remembered, at least by your children. But the rhythms and patterns developed right now, for better or worse, continue on forever.

Patterns For Breakfast Translate Patterns For Life

Our natural inclination is to grab some cheerios, put them in a bowl, shove them into our child's hands, turn on the TV, and climb back into bed. While you are accomplishing the practical act of breakfast, you are missing the sacred act of breakfast. The sad reality is that we (okay, *I*) so often sacrifice sacred moments for a few more minutes of sleep or a baseball game. And these fleeting moments accumulate to the point that we have set in stone certain patterns of interacting that are very difficult to change.

The patterns we set up and create, for better or for worse, stay with us forever. I thought it was cute that my son didn't eat cereal with milk or a spoon, and so to this day he still eats with his cereal with his hands. No amount of peer pressure or parental shame has helped him eat like 99% of the other boys in the world. I thought it would be easier to just put on the TV for a half hour so I could get a little more sleep, and it was almost World War III when we realized that sort of stimulant just created cranky attitudes and took away some much needed interaction time.

While Cheerios in front of TV provides nourishment to the body, it provides absolutely nothing for their souls. Cheerios don't smell, they barely taste, and because of that they don't stick in our memories. The sense of smell is one of the most powerful triggers for our memories. And a breakfast meal has a very unique and strong smell. In our house, the tradition is sausage and pancakes. With just a little bit of intention, and in a matter of a couple of weeks, we transformed the morning rhythm of our home. In the dawn of the morning, our house is beginning to develop a distinct character; the taste of coffee, the crackle of the sausage, and the unique smell pancakes have cooking on my grandmother's cast iron griddle.

These tastes and smells, combined with the reality of us sitting together as a family, looking at each other, and interacting, are creating deep pathways for memories of value and love between our children and us. The simple act of saying grace and attempting a family question sets patterns for prayer and interaction that cereal in front of the television can never replicate.

For good and for bad, the patterns we create right now compound on themselves, either creating deep and fond memories for our kids, or sending a subtle, low-level communication to them that the easy road, at the expense of memorable experiences, is always the way to go. My wife and I have wrestled with this reality, celebrating success, and our failures (well, that is what new mercies are for!), every day. You know, it is incredibly hard to not take the easy path with every moment of life. So how can we lean more fully into this sacred space of breakfast? Before we move on, it might be a good idea for you to grab one more cup of coffee.

We have to forget about the fleeting value of sleep and efficiency, and lean into the reality that breakfast is a sacred meal, and the breakfast table is sacred space. This reality shapes our hearts, which then shapes our days, which it turn shapes our lives.

True Communion

Throughout all of scripture we see that sharing a meal together is one of the most sacred of events. Yes, scripture does not record every meal and, for sure, doesn't record the mayhem of breakfast with toddlers. But it does record the significance meals can have. The most significant Jewish meal has been and still is today the Passover. It was a regular meal eaten before an amazing event. And to this day, Jewish families gather to celebrate the Passover meal where they tell the story of God rescuing His people out of slavery and bringing them to the Promised Land. In this sacred meal, the youngest person at the table traditionally asks the four framing questions, beginning with, "Why is this night different from all other nights?"

Jewish tradition has it right. We gather for meals and our meals have purpose. Often they are ordinary and plain. Instead of simply working through logistics and calling that conversation, we have the opportunities to create family questions that work both right now with little ones, and create patterns for communication that will be set for years to come. Family questions allow space for everyone to share their lives, their joys, their concerns, their faith, and their struggles. And when significant holidays, joyous celebrations, and tragic events occur, there is a natural rhythm and place to land to retell the family story, to affirm our faith, and to walk through life on a united front.

Jesus took the Passover meal and added depth and meaning when He transformed it into communion; the sacred meal the church celebrates as we remember the life, death and resurrection of Jesus Christ. In a dramatic way, Jesus took a familiar meal, which had already been made special through the Passover tradition, and added to the mix the spiritual nourishment needed to live the full and abundant life. In a less dramatic way, we get to lean into this every breakfast, and actually, every mealtime.

It doesn't take much reflection to realize that in neutral, our lives are broken and scattered. We are wounded and separated from each other and God because of the dumb choices we have made and the dumber choices others have made towards us. The Eucharist is a meal where the people of God gather together and remember that Jesus took our brokenness upon Himself, and that He nourishes us as the bread of life.

It is a meal where Jesus chooses to communicate His most significant teachings.

The breakfast story hardly seems this dramatic. But over the long haul, the breakfast story actually becomes the place for our most dramatic and significant teachings. It is the breakfast table where we communicate our family's deepest values in a tactile way. It is the breakfast table where we are nourished and reminded of God's goodness and blessing to our family. It is at the breakfast table where we intentionally check in with one another, forgive one another of our dumb choices and hurtful actions and words. It is the breakfast table where we are loved, connected, nourished, and ultimately sent into the day and into the world.

May breakfast become the most important meal for your body and your soul.

Questions for Reflection:
1) When is the meal that your entire family can be together around the table?

2) What sorts of traditions do you remember from your childhood and find value in today?

3) What are some things that you can do to make meal times more sacred?

chapter three: BUILDING BLOCKS AND TEA PARTIES BEING PRESENT

Did You See My Status?

The other night we had a pool party with the middle school group from my church. While people were arriving, the girl who lives at the house ran outside to show the gathering crowd and me her birthday present. To our amazement and delight, she revealed a life-sized, Justin Bieber cardboard cutout. Instantly the cameras came out and the line was formed. As the adult in the group I tried to play it cool. But soon enough it was my turn to stand next to Justin and pose for the picture, and it was only a moment later that I uploaded that picture to Facebook with a clever comment.

Almost instantly, my Facebook page began to blow up. It seemed like every minute someone was pressing the "like" button or adding a funny comment of their own. What I found interesting was that my job and focus was supposed to be at the junior high pool party, hanging out with students and staff, being present with them, loving them and encouraging them, but instead I found myself continually checking my Facebook notifications to enjoy the stream of comments.

It is surprising that as fast as technology is changing and seemingly changing us, the core of who we are never changes. We are human beings who have an inner desire to be seen and known. For parents, with a hectic job and life, a lot of that, for better or worse, comes through social media and texting. When we post a picture or comment and people notice that and comment on that, something inside of us grows. We are no longer just objects taking up space, but there is an interaction and affirmation of our existence.

I don't think social media is the end-all be-all to being known, but it does seem to scratch that itch. It also seems to be reforming social etiquette. Eye contact and undivided attention are now optional. While this may be all right with us adults, our children begin to miss out on the amazing gift of being known.

Being seen and known is vital to our existence as humans. Our children need this affirmation much more. The way our children understand that they are valued and known is not by comments on their Facebook photos, but by us-- their parents--speaking their love language. And for most toddlers, the way that they receive love is through parents getting on the floor, on their level, and playing with them. Playing with the toys and the games they enjoy. Sharing in stacking blocks, lining up race cars, building forts, reading books, and having tea parties, is really a form of communication to our kids.

In the same way an affirmation of our clever Facebook posts builds us up because we feel seen, playing games and having tea parties builds our children up. Because social media has not ruined them yet, they for another year or so are part of the old school. They receive love and affirmation the way humans have done it for thousands and thousands of years, eye contact, interaction, play, and conversation.

The challenge is that doing these things with a toddler seems belittling to us and takes up too much time. We are important people with places to go and errands to run. If our kids were in charge we would just sit down and play all morning together. Instead of running off to the gym or the store, maybe this morning you could practice the spiritual discipline of presence, the simple act of being with someone else, with no agenda, reflecting love and affirmation.

This is so far from our normal rhythm of life that it actually feels unnatural. But that is a symptom of our brokenness, more than a sign of it not being worthwhile. In order to really soak this up with our kids and even with our walk with God, we have to get over our own issues, be intentional with our time, and relearn eye contact.

I Used To Be a Professional

I distinctly remember coming home from work one day all excited about a couple of new projects I had been working on. In contrast, my wife was having a down day. Because I don't really pick up on the subtleties of her emotional state of being, she had to make it clear to me what she had been going through that day.

The kids were finally in bed, and we were sitting on the couch enjoying a glass of wine, when she interrupted the retelling of my amazing day with an unexpectedly firm question. "Do you want to know what I did all day?" Because I was just now starting to realize something was up, I prepared to hear about all the horror of the day with diaper disasters and temper-tantrums. But to my surprise, she told a completely different story.

"For three hours today I sat on the floor and lined up cars from one side of our living room to the other!" I didn't really understand why that statement needed an exclamation point, so I followed up with a simple question about why that was such a bad thing.

For the next hour or so, my wife processed the melancholy she was experiencing. She had been a respected teacher for years. She had colleagues, a desk, a paycheck. Her students and the administration valued her. And now, her once-full days of being a contributor were sucked away by seemingly inconsequential tasks and boring games. Not being mentally stimulated or contributing in the manner in which she used to had begun to take a toll.

I start to feel this way in just a matter of minutes when I am having a tea party with my daughter. But even on days when I am all-in with my kids, Monday eventually comes around and I get to go back to work. Monday never comes for my wife. Unless we come to grips with this loss and reframe our playtime, we will never get down on the floor again. Our kids need us to be present and be on their level, and that often means that we are the ones (in our case my wife is most often the one), who must die to the old self, and for the sake of the emotional development of our children, put the phone away, turn off the TV, and line up cars and have tea parties with our kids.

Be Intentional With Your Time

Pulling this off really isn't as difficult as we make it. We have gotten to be very good at filling our days with seemingly important tasks, and limiting our actual free time with many distractions. To live into this spiritual discipline of presence, it is really as simple as being intentional with our time.

For me, I spent just one day thinking about what I really do with my time. When I was home, I realized, my phone, Facebook, my computer, the TV took up the little margins in my time and conversations. My interaction became transactional with my kids and even with my wife.

A simple discipline I am starting to do is to put my phone away when I get home from work and not check it again until the kids are asleep. This one change has greatly expanded the margins in my day. We all have little and big things we do with our free moments; the trick is simply using those free moments with intention. With the TV off and the phone put away, I am now forced to be creative and interact with my kids, and to do so on their level.

Because toddlers can't text yet, we have to communicate love in a way that makes sense to them. We have to walk at their pace. And for better or worse, their pace is slow and boring for us. But the benefit to their soul is immeasurable. It would be an awful thing to ingrain in the psyche of our children that our computers and phones are more important to us than the actual interaction and presence of our children. We may not even be workaholics, but technology can fill that place just as well. Just like that old song, *The Cat's in the Cradle*, we will reap what we sow relationally with our kids, and the rhythms of this begin now.

Relearn Eye Contact

We adults are quickly forgetting the art of giving someone your undivided attention. It has become normal for us to only partially engage while we do some other task. But when we do this we start to lose some of our humanness. Being seen, and being known is one of our core needs. This is communicated to us by others being present with us, with others stopping what they are doing and noticing us, engaging us. We have allowed silly Facebook comments to take this place for us, but that's only a shadow of the real deal.

Our kids will only have this need met if we are actually present with them. This simply means that we have to turn off the distractions in our lives and give them our eye contact, our undivided attention, and speak their love languages. Right now, our task is to die to our own junk and selflessly give our kids our presence. This often takes us turning off our shows, getting on the carpet and oozing love and affection onto our kids.

This is also true in our walk with God. We think it is difficult to give up a couple of hours and do nothing productive while we play with our kids--our very own offspring. The truth is, it is way more difficult to put away the many distractions in our lives, give up precious sleep or the need to be productive, and make space to soak up the presence of God.

We too are helpless children who are in desperate need of love and affection, and God is our parent who is never too busy or distracted to get down onto our level and care for us. We are totally seen by Him, totally understood, and totally loved. We often miss this because we are too busy updating our Facebook status rather then dying to our distractions, being intentional with our time, and actually giving our undivided attention to the One who created us, loves us, and leads us.

As we nurture our relationships with our children through the discipline of presence, may we be just as intentional making space for the presence of God in our lives. May we be open for God to search us, know us, and test us, so that God may point out anything in us that offends Him or others, and truly lead us along the path of everlasting life!

The Gift of Presence: Psalm 139 (NLT)

1 O Lord, you have examined my heart
and know everything about me.
2 You know when I sit down or stand up.
You know my thoughts even when I'm far away.
3 You see me when I travel
and when I rest at home.
You know everything I do.
4 You know what I am going to say
even before I say it, Lord.
5 You go before me and follow me.
You place your hand of blessing on my head.
6 Such knowledge is too wonderful for me,
too great for me to understand!
7 I can never escape from your Spirit!
I can never get away from your presence!
8 If I go up to heaven, you are there;
if I go down to the grave,[a] you are there.
9 If I ride the wings of the morning,
if I dwell by the farthest oceans,
10 even there your hand will guide me,
and your strength will support me.
11 I could ask the darkness to hide me
and the light around me to become night—
12 but even in darkness I cannot hide from you.

To you the night shines as bright as day.
  Darkness and light are the same to you.

13 You made all the delicate, inner parts of my body
  and knit me together in my mother's womb.
14 Thank you for making me so wonderfully complex!
  Your workmanship is marvelous—how well I know it.
15 You watched me as I was being formed in utter seclusion,
  as I was woven together in the dark of the womb.
16 You saw me before I was born.
  Every day of my life was recorded in your book.
 Every moment was laid out
  before a single day had passed.

17 How precious are your thoughts about me,[b] O God.
  They cannot be numbered!
18 I can't even count them;
  they outnumber the grains of sand!
 And when I wake up,
  you are still with me!

19 O God, if only you would destroy the wicked!
  Get out of my life, you murderers!
20 They blaspheme you;
  your enemies misuse your name.
21 O Lord, shouldn't I hate those who hate you?
  Shouldn't I despise those who oppose you?
22 Yes, I hate them with total hatred,
  for your enemies are my enemies.

23 Search me, O God, and know my heart;
  test me and know my anxious thoughts.
24 Point out anything in me that offends you,
  and lead me along the path of everlasting life.

Questions for Reflection:

1) What are the distractions that suck up the margins in your free time?
2) What activities allow you to be most present with your child?
3) Take 10 minutes to be quiet and present with God. Pray through Psalm 139, and allow for some quiet so God can answer the questions posed in verses 23 and 24.

chapter four: PLAY DATES:
THE BEGINNING OF COMMUNITY

My Daughter is Perfect

My daughter is the apple of my eye. I seriously think she can do no wrong. She is silly and sweet. She is adventuresome and fearless. She hosts the most amazing tea parties on the planet, and loves hip hop music. However I tease her, she teases me right back. I am mesmerized by her cuteness.

But being mesmerized has blinded my ability to parent. Because she can do no wrong with me, there has to be some other person to blame when trouble breaks out. Unfortunately, my son bears the brunt of this responsibility. He is three years older than she is. He is bigger than she is, smarter than she is, and more responsible than she is. So when a fight erupts, my instinct is to defend my daughter and come down on my son.

Thankfully these little eruptions are few and far between. Most of the reason for this is that they are in completely different stages of development, enjoy doing different things, and play with completely different toys. But inevitably the poking and wrestling goes south and someone ends up crying. At which point I naturally default to blaming my son.

No matter how close your kids are in age, or if they have other siblings at all, the truth is that our kids are not as perfect, brilliant, or sweet as we think. All parents have blind spots when it comes to our view of our kids, how we parent, and how we discipline. I am sure there are worthy books full of research as to the why of this phenomenon, but the why is not what is important. Finding our blind spots so we can develop children who are kind and thoughtful, who have character and faith, is the vital and difficult task.

As I've said, I have an awful blind spot when it comes to my daughter, and this blind spot isn't fair for my son. It puts an unnecessary burden of responsibility on him, and actually crushes his spirit when I'm blindly defending my daughter. And it isn't helpful for my daughter's development as I am subtly teaching her she is the center of the universe and can really do no wrong.

Thankfully we have found a way to shed our blinders: play dates. Now, we didn't start having play dates for our kids as a developmental tool. We simply wanted some help with childcare and to keep our kids occupied so we could get some work done around the house. Sharing kids meant some time away from them for errands, the gym, or to simply kick back and read a book. While they may have started out as breaks for my wife and I, they have turned out to be the single most helpful tool to reveal the character flaws and selfishness in our own kids.

A Play Date Gone South

It was just a year ago when a family in our church offered to have a play date with our daughter. This was a great break for us. But when we picked up our daughter, the mom shared with us that the girls struggled a little bit in their interaction. We figured this was normal, and set up a date to return the favor. In the next couple of weeks, their daughter came to our house to play, and we got to fully see what "struggled a little bit" really meant. It was a disaster!

These two girls spent most of the play date "together" being separated, and my daughter spent most of the time being in trouble. They fought over everything: every decision, every toy, every snack, every costume, every conversation. These two youngest girls, in families of older brothers, had never had to share dresses before, and it didn't go well.

After a couple of hours, the other girl finally went home and my wife and I debriefed the situation like people who were suffering from post-traumatic stress. And what I kept coming back to was my daughter really isn't as sweet and funny as I thought she was. She was actually a spoiled brat who couldn't share to save her life. The blinders were finally coming off. It was time for me to swallow the hard truth that I had favored my baby girl and in the process created a monster. With the problem in front of me, I had to wrestle with the solution.

I realized that the solution to my daughter's character flaws might actually be the same thing that revealed these flaws to me in the first place. Instead of fewer play dates because they were disasters, she needed more of them to refine her character and create opportunities to shape her behavior.

The Loss of Community

When we live isolated lives, we develop a worldview that keeps us at the center. We get so used to expecting everything to go our way that we often forget there are many other options and ways than "our way." An isolated life also atrophies our ability to relate well with others. What we think is silly and clever really comes off as selfish and rude.

The solution to this problem has been a part of our DNA since the beginning of time. Living life together in community is the number one way our character is properly formed. For all of human history people have lived together in community, sharing lives and resources with one another, and as they do their true character gets revealed to the entire world.

We were created in the image of the triune God. God's very character and nature is one of community. Some theologians have actually referred to the Trinity--Father, Son, Holy Ghost--as the true community of Love. Three persons, one God. Because we were made in the image of God, our very being longs to be in community with God and with others. We actually live life to be connected with other people. It is because of this nature that the worst form of punishment for us is forced isolation, and for our kids, time-outs.

For the first time ever, authentic community is an option in our culture. Our entire lives can be, and often are, lived in isolation from others. We are completely self-sufficient in our resources, our entertainment, and even in our interactions with others. Facebook and texting give us adults the sense that we are connected to others, but without any of the emotional cost of having to actually interact, make eye contact, listen, and share with someone else. And because of this, our entire character as a culture is getting more and more selfish and self-absorbed.

We for sure have our own blinders on regarding how selfish and self-absorbed we are. But for me, that is a little tough to swallow. I can barely identify that my own kids are that way. Whether it is my children, or myself, the way we refine our fallen character is by developing community.

Play Dates: The Beginning of Community

It is sometimes easy to think keeping our children in isolation, under our direct care and supervision, does an adequate job of developing our children's character. As least for me, this presupposition ends up being false, and solidifies my own blind spots about my children. Our children are just human as we are and in just as much need of community. Community for our children builds them up, as well as revealing areas needing growth and development.

Play dates are the beginning of community for our children. Being built up and loved on by us, their parents, is an incredible gift. But learning how to interact and succeed with others is what will solidify their self-esteem and identity. As our children grow up they will know that we love them. We are supposed to love them. Later on, the question will be whether or not *others* love them.

Building friendships and community may be part of our DNA, but it is still a learned activity, and playing with other kids their age is where this learning starts.

Building community happens by putting into place the most famous rule in all of scripture, the Golden Rule. Matthew 22:39 tells us, "Love your neighbor as yourself." We all want to be treated with respect. We want to be seen and not taken for granted. We want to be heard and cared for. Just because these are *our* desires doesn't mean we know to do this for others. Putting others above ourselves--sharing, listening, serving, inviting--are things that don't come naturally, but must be learned. And these are lessons learned when we rub shoulders with other people in community.

Play dates are the place where our kids get to put into practice all the lessons we've been teaching them. Talking about manners and sharing is mostly academic in our own households. When our children play with other kids, the rubber meets the road and we see how much of what we've taught has actually been learned. We can think that our kids excel in these things, but when we see them play with their peers we realize how much more work there is to be done. If your kids are anything like mine, it only takes a couple of interactions to see that what I thought I'd been teaching has not sunk in, and the blinders I once had are quickly falling off due to the embarrassment of my perfect angel behaving so badly.

I get so used to the rhythms of interaction within my family and the idiosyncrasies of each child that it's easy for me to think all is well. The exact same thing is true in my own life, in my own interactions with others. It's when I rub up with someone else, and don't get my way or have conflict that I have the opportunity to have my rough edges ground off. When there is conflict with another person, or between my child and their play date, my first inclination is to defend and rationalize behavior. But this only keeps the blinders on and doesn't do anything to soften our hearts or develop character.

It is a difficult experiment to see the experiences and interactions our child has during a play date as an evaluation for the character development that is happening inside her. Instead of trying to defend every poor choice or rescue a difficult encounter, we have the opportunity to use every interaction as a teachable moment.

We Choose Our Community For Our Kids

We often think that community just happens out of thin air. While it is in our DNA to be in community, it is getting more and more difficult to connect our lives in an intentional, meaningful way. This is even more true with our kids. If we hand over to our children complete control of the community of friends they are going to have, they will find themselves in big trouble.

The truth is that we as parents should 100% choose the community for our children while they are still under our full control and supervision. Since this is the case, we have the opportunity to help our children develop friendships with kids whose parents are people we like to be around, who share the same values, and who will help our children develop character and learn to interact well with others. Ideally, these play dates are the beginning of community for our kids and will begin to develop the habits, manners, and character that will lay the foundation for long-term friendship and community.

As important as it is for our children to put their character to the test by interacting with others in community, the same is true for us adults. By being isolated people who have few friendships, and fewer friendships that help shape our soul, we become people who get more and more spiritually dull. As the author of Proverbs says, "As iron sharpens iron, so a friend sharpens a friend" (Proverbs 27:17). It is life in community that helps us take our blinders off and reveals to us our true character. We are to be people who are deeply connected to one another, people who love, care for, and serve one another. And unless we actually have others in our lives we will never be able to fulfill the second of the two greatest commandments.

Questions for Reflection:
1) What are some of the blind spots you may have regarding your own children and their behavior?
2) Who are some families in your life who would be a benefit to your children's character development?
3) Who are some people in your life with whom you can build some more intentional community?

chapter five: NAP TIME = REST TIME

The Creation Story

"In the beginning God created the heavens and the earth" (Genesis 1:1). This is how the story of scripture begins: God at work creating all things, all things new and all things good; the heavens, the earth, the waters and the land, the animals in the water and the animals on land. And finally, God created the pinnacle of creation, humans; made not just by God, but in the image of God, a reflection of His very character. Then, after all the dramatic events of six full days of work, God rested. Scripture says, "By the seventh day God had finished the work He had been doing; so on the seventh day He rested from all His work" (Genesis 2:2).

In the very character of God is all of this desire to work and create, to be productive. This was instilled in humanity when we were made in His image. And just like we were created to work and be productive, we were also made to rest. If God rested from all of His work, then we, being made in His image, need to rest too.

Resting is so important to the character of God and for us who are created in His image that scripture goes on to teach how God set apart the seventh day and made it holy; set it apart as a day of rest. And if this wasn't clear enough, God even etched it into stone on the tablets of the Ten Commandments. Exodus 20:8-10 says, "Remember the Sabbath day by keeping it holy. Six days you shall labor and do all your work, but the seventh day is Sabbath to the Lord your God. On it you shall not do any work."

Sabbath rest is by far the most forgotten aspect to our spiritual lives. We live in such a fast-paced world, where productivity is honored above all else, that we pass right over this important principle. And actually, it isn't really a principle at all--it is a *commandment*. Thankfully our little guys help us live into this discipline, because they intuitively know they need to rest and do it. So should we.

You Are Busy

Last summer I went camping along the Russian River with my family. My desire was to spend a weekend away with my family with no agenda other than sit by the river with my feet in the water enjoying a book and the presence of my family all together. No cell phones, no tasks to accomplish, just us building memories.

First of all, camping with little ones is not relaxing in the slightest, and all of my expectations were not met. But that's another book. While my family and I were unpacking the massive amount of beach gear and started to make our way toward the water's edge, I saw something that caught my attention.

Down by the water was a group of high school or college kids having the time of their lives. They were barbecuing, throwing a frisbee, splashing in the water, and laughing. In fact that was what stuck out to me the most. What in the world could be so funny as to keep this group laughing for hours at a time? It was such a stark contrast to my family's adventure. We had to make sure our kids were safe, had on their life jackets, sun screen, snacks, all while being in close proximity to the bathrooms. There was significantly less laughing on our side of the beach.

Remember when life was that simple? You went and did the things you wanted to do, when you wanted to do them. Road-trip? Let's go. Hungry? Let's eat. Not a care in the world. But those days are long gone. Now we are responsible for little lives. Life is busy and full, and even days off don't feel like days off. Sometimes I have found that going to work is more relaxing than family time!

We work hard at providing a good life for our kids. We work at jobs that are demanding and take an incredible amount of mental energy as we work our way up the corporate ladder. Or we stay home and manage a household that is in a constant state of disarray. A complaint my wife often has is that she is exhausted at the end of the day and all she has to show for herself is that the laundry is done and there is food in the fridge, only to all end up in disarray again tomorrow. We are full, emotionally and physically. We are in need of rest!

Our Kids Get It

Everyone needs rest. We were created to work hard for a time and then rest. Rest is often the first thing prescribed by doctors when we are sick or even break our bones. Casts force our bones to rest. And when we rest, healing and restoration happens. It is how we were made.

What I love about kids is that they get it. Kids seem to run at a million miles an hour. They go, go, go, go. But then they just stop. Some of my favorite YouTube videos are kids falling asleep in the strangest places. They just crash out in cars, in church, in shopping carts, and even while throwing a temper-tantrum. The most common place seems to be in high chairs during a meal. I don't get this at all. Meals are a core value for me, but for some kids, it doesn't matter where they are. If they are tired, the face goes into the spaghetti.

Our kids need to rest. Most kids need 12 hours at night and a couple of hours in the middle of the day. Every child is different, but any way you cut it they need way more sleep then we do. At least they need more sleep then we *get*.

I remember traveling with our little kids. In order to get to our destination in time, we had to travel through naptime, and then we didn't even arrive until after bedtime. By the time we got settled and had a meal, our kids were way overdue on sleep. It didn't seem to matter so much during our trip that day, but because we had made this mistake before, we knew that the next day was going to be rough. And sure enough, from the time the sun rose, our kids were crabby, whiny, and a challenge to be around. This is because their tank was empty. They need rest to function correctly and we deprived them of that.

We Need Rest Too

Unfortunately, I order my adult life in a similar way to that road trip. I power through to get done all that needs to get done. I am in a season professionally where advancement is there for the taking. Other parents in this season of life are experiencing a similar draw. During this time in our careers there are more and more opportunities to climb the ladder to bigger and better options professionally. But when you add the additional stresses and demands at work, plus the increasing needs of the family, and try to squeeze in a couple of things for you personally, there is zero time left. The first thing to go, when trying to manage all these responsibilities, is sleep and rest for sure. Before I know it, I am the one who is crabby, whiny, and a challenge to be around.

My wife experiences the same rat race trying to maintain our home and complete the tasks of her part-time job. The worst part is that her rat race feels more like a rat wheel. All of the tasks that she completes only prepare her to do the exact same ones the next day. Doing laundry, going shopping, and picking up after the whirlwind of toddlers is exhausting, and not satisfying.

It is an awful feeling to finally get the kids down to bed, clean up the house, finish your last bit of work responsibilities, prepare the house for tomorrow, and sit down on the couch, only to be so exhausted from the day that you have nothing left. Not even enough to enjoy one of your favorite shows.

It Doesn't Have To Be Like This

The types of days described above are depressing, and can make you feel hopeless. To combat this relentless rat race, at our house we have instituted some strict sleep-time boundaries. Our little ones need at least 12 hours of sleep a night and a couple hours of sleep during the day. And even when they outgrow their naps, the 12 hours a night is recommended all the way into elementary school.

7:00 PM has become the most important time in our day. It is the time when our kids go to bed, whether they are ready for it or not. By 7:00 they have bathed, prayed, and are told to stay in their rooms. This rest is good for them, but has turned out to be vital for us. From 7:00 to bedtime for us, our house is quiet, and we have time to connect and relax together. Even after spending an hour or so getting things in order for the next day, we still have a couple of hours to read, watch television, and visit.

Naptime has proven to be a vital time as well. This two-hour chunk of time makes or breaks our kids' attitude for the rest of the day. This should be a great reminder for us as well. The easiest thing is using naptime (or what transitions to "quiet time" as the kids get older and naps fade), to run around the house and tie up loose ends. Maybe a better choice is to follow the lead of our children and get some rest ourselves. Rest can mean a variety of things based on what your body and soul need. Scripture is clear that we are to rest; our job is to find the things that actually allow us to do that.

Besides a day of Sabbath rest, we need to develop a lifestyle of rest. Being busy and strung out from working so hard in and out of the home are not the things that our kids are going to want to remember about us. They are going to want to remember their parents as people who are present and love and care for them. It is impossible to give our kids what they need emotionally and spiritually if we are exhausted and stressed, and don't have anything to give.

When we are rested, our fuses are longer and we have all the space in the world to be together as a family. Our kids are such a great reminder of this truth. When they do not get enough rest they are impossible to be around. I think the same is true for us. We may think nobody notices how exhausted we really are, but intuitively our kids get that we are stressed and not really present. Maybe we are not as developed and mature as we think we are. We are in need of rest, not because we are weak, but because we are made in the very nature of God. Since God rested, so should we.

Rest Is My Favorite Spiritual Discipline

It is a discipline that God Himself does.

It is a discipline that actually fills a real human need.

It is a discipline that fills us for the activity to follow.

We are consumed with being busy and active. But for this tiny window in the life of our child, maybe we too can soak up--guilt-free--the discipline and sacrament of rest!

Questions for Reflection:
1) How many hours of sleep do your kids get? How much sleep do you get?
2) On a scale of 1-10 how short is your fuse with your kids, your spouse? How much does rest affect this number?
3) What needs to change in the rhythm of your life to make space for weekly rest, and even daily rest?

chapter six: CAR TIME: PRAYING WITHOUT CEASING

How Many Words Do You Say?

Have you ever heard of the urban legend about how many words men and women speak in a day? It states that women speak an average of 20,000 words a day while men speak an average of 7,000. This seems to make a lot of sense, especially when a husband and wife are reunited at the end of the day and the husband is ready to check out while the wife seems to have a never-ending flow of words.

It turns out that this is just an anecdotal story a marriage counselor shared with his patients, which caught some momentum and has now become part of the urban legend foundation of how we think about communication. But the truth is, a short Google search finds that both men and women speak between 7,000 and 9,000 words in a day.

More than the numbers of words that are spoken in a day, I have become intrigued by the ways in which these words are spoken. When I think of top-shelf communication, I imagine leaving my kids with a baby sitter and taking my wife to our favorite steak house. We usually get there a half hour before our reservation and enjoy a fancy cocktail in the bar. Before long, our names are called, and we are ushered back to our private booth in the back of the restaurant.

Over the next two hours or so, we enjoy appetizers, salads, steaks, and some insanely, decadent dessert with some coffee. It is in this setting, over these hours, that some of the most important conversations happen. It is here where we evaluate our parenting, reflect on our marriage, examine our faith, laugh at silly things our kids have done and sometimes even shed some tears about the difficult times in which we find ourselves. This is real communication.

How often do these conversations really happen? In the midst of a crazy life with a million plates in the air that must all remain spinning, these precious conversations are few and far between. The truth is that there seem to be many different levels of conversation that happen throughout the day and week.

Our Typical Conversations

There is the morning check-in. Until we started being more intentional with our breakfast time, this was the time of day where I get ready to head out the door to work, our kids are waking up, and we are trying to get our son off to school. This usually is the time where we work out the logistics, the details, who is picking up who and when. There are very few touchy-feelys here.

There is the mid-day phone check in. I have found that these too are rarely touchy-feely. More logistics, the ones that we have forgotten about and must be worked out. Often these conversations are sprinkled with sharing about mid-day drama at work or with the kids. Every now and then, a funny story about something silly a kid says makes its way into these times.

There are the get-home and get-to-it conversations: These are my least favorite conversations of the day. My wife is fried from being with the kids and recovering from the many different blow-ups that occurred throughout the day, and I haven't fully settled down from a long day at work. But the second I come through the door it is go time: dinner, reading, baths and bedtime. It is actually an amazing dance where we intuitively pass kids back and forth calling out plays like a quarterback does in a non-huddle offense.

There are the post-bedtime conversations: These are really a mixed bag. Sometimes they are intentional times where we get to talk about the deeper things of life, and often they include the two of us using non-verbal communication as we soak up some well-deserved quiet and rest.

Besides the typical times of communication, we have other kinds scattered throughout our day and week. At least once a week we try to ditch the kids and go to Starbucks for an hour or so, to remind ourselves that we are married and have a relationship. It is amazing how good an hour feels in the midst of a chaotic week and a chaotic life.

Who Talks Like This?

Of all the words I use up in a day, I have found that very few of them are across the table listening and speaking. Rarely do I have a cup of coffee in my hand, no distractions around, and I can fully engage the person I am with.

The more I've thought about this, the more I have started to notice that very rarely does anyone have intentional, sit-down, uninterrupted discussions. In fact, I don't know any men who do this, and I definitely don't know any kids who do this. Actually, it seems to be only adult women, and adult women who are post-toddler stage who actually sit down and talk with this kind of intention.

Which leads me to my main point: No one sits down and has intentional conversation, face-to-face. OK, this might be a little dramatic, but it sure seems to be rare. Next time you go into Starbucks, look around and see who is there to just have coffee and visit with a friend. Who ever it is, it definitely isn't moms with preschoolers.

Most Conversations are Spent In Transition

While the dream is for us to have our 7,000 - 9,000 words be used in intentional conversation around a cup of coffee, the truth is that most of our words are used up in the in-between times. This isn't necessarily a bad thing, it just is. But if this reality is also a reality for you too, then the important question is, how do we use these in-between times with a little more intention and purpose?

This reality becomes even more important when it comes to how we have conversations with our kids. And this reality becomes vital when it comes to the things we want to communicate to our kids and make sure they understand.

Before I really thought this through I came up with a great plan for us to have intentional family conversations. For our family, breakfast seems to be the one constant time in the day where we are all awake and present. So, I decided I was going to capitalize on this time we were all together and institute a family question. The problem is that for a day or so, I forgot that I had two children under 5, not other adults.

Day one: pancakes cooked up, orange juice poured, and grace said. It was now time for the important family conversation. I cleared my throat, took a sip of coffee and asked my kids, what was something they learned in Sunday School yesterday? So far, so good.

Before my son could even get one sentence out of his mouth, my daughter spilled her juice into my son's breakfast. At this point, everything went into slow motion. My daughter began to cry as the juice spilled on to her nightgown. My son got mad because some of the juice landed on his pancakes. So he yelled at his sister, giving her a piece of his mind. This made her cry even more. This spiraling scene caused complete regression in me and I yelled at both of my kids. Within 60 seconds everyone, including the dog, were crying and my wife just sat there, shaking her head. So close. We had been so close!

Taking Advantage of Our Natural Points of Conversation

After the disaster at the breakfast table, my wife reminded me that we had little kids, and no little kids sit down and discuss life over breakfast. In fact anyone who works with children knows that the best way to get kids to talk is to not actually sit and stare at them while you ask questions. The way is to play together, draw together, and while in activity, let conversation result naturally.

When I started to think about it, I realized that I actually had a lot of time with my kids where we are in transition-

-running around town, taking care of family business. While they were strapped in their car seats, there was nowhere for them to go, and nothing for them to do except talk.

We decided that our trips around town could be so much more than just errands where we drag our kids form one store to the next. Those transitions could actually be some of the times and places where we connected with our kids and found out what sort of things were rumbling around in their heads. It was amazing what sort of answers came out of their mouths when they didn't feel me staring them down, and they had space to look at books and play with stickers while we talked.

So now, it is in our car rides that we ask our kids about their Sunday School lessons, talk about what songs mean, who we are praying for, how beautiful creation is, how much we love our family and our church family. Our car rides are where we take care of business. The most significant conversations we have with our kids often happen as we drive from there to here, or play on the floor building Legos, or take walks around the neighborhood.

Since those intimate conversations around the dinner table or at Starbucks are not going to happen for the foreseeable future with our kids, we found we have to take advantage of the in-between times. If we don't, we'll miss out on years of conversation and teachable moments. It is too bad that we think unless conversations look and feel a certain way they aren't important or valuable. But almost all of the conversations we have, whether they are with our spouse, our kids, our friends, or our co-workers, happen in the moments we find ourselves between tasks, running from here to there.

Maybe We Can Pray Without Ceasing

I wonder if this same reality could be true in our walk with God. I think Brother Lawrence would say so. I often think that the only conversations that matter with God are the ones where I can manage to wake myself up extra early, before my kids, make some coffee, and have some intentional prayer.

But if my prayer time only consists of these few and far between perfectly serene, quiet times, then I will miss out on many important conversations with God through my day and week. When Paul talks about praying without ceasing in 1 Thessalonians, maybe Paul wasn't talking about a prayer life that one never-ending quiet time that only monks or ascetics can pull off.

These intentional quiet times are important and needed, just like sharing over cups of coffee are with my wife. Yes, the very intentional space for spiritual growth is also important, just like the special dinners at the steakhouse. Without these times of reflection and sharing, our faith will become stunted and stagnate. But just as important are the in-between times of our lives, the transition times, as we move from place to place, task to task. I wonder if God appreciates being a part of our thought life throughout our day as we walk through big and small decisions, as we celebrate victories and defeats, as we cuddle with our kids and lose our tempers. I would bet He does.

Staying connected with God throughout the day keeps us on our spiritual toes and keeps our hearts tuned to the things of God. By intentionally connecting with God in the transitions, we are reminded that we need to be connected with our spouse in these times as well. And, being connected to God in the transition reminds us that transitions are actually sacred space, where we can have deep and meaningful conversations with our kids as we help them develop their faith and love God.

Questions For Reflection:
1) Where do you go to have intentional conversations with your spouse?
2) Where do you go to have intentional conversations with God?
3) How would you rate your transition conversations with your spouse and with God?
4) Where is an in-between time you can have more intentional conversation with your kids?

chapter seven: STRANGER DANGER: DEVELOPING DISCERNMENT

Going to the Park

In the town where I grew up, my friends and I had a favorite park. It was called Pioneer Park, and among all the different parks in our area, this one was by far the best. It had a large lawn that was sloped, perfect for rolling down. There was a huge play structure built in a way where we could not only climb it, but had a top level covering that, if we were brave enough, we could shimmy our way onto and see the entire park.

Besides the play structure and the lawn, there was an old, dry cement-lined pond we could ride our bikes through, and behind that was the creek. In the creek were crawdads, spiders, and even snakes. And the best part was a creepy old cemetery attached to the park where we would play hide and seek and try to freak each other out. Basically this park had it all. There were baby swings for my sister, and the entire rest of the park for me and my buddies to spend hours running, playing, falling down and getting back up.

After I grew up and moved away, this park turned into legend status for me. It was a marker of my childhood, and has continued to hold deep and fond memories for me. So when my kids were old enough, I couldn't wait to take them to this park, and pass on this place that was so rich for me to the next generation. With eager anticipation, we packed a blanket, some food, water bottles, and our kids, and away we drove.

The second I got out of the car, everything seemed different. I quickly scanned the park and as the sign clearly said, and the basic contours of the landscape reminded me, this was in fact Pioneer Park. There was the cemetery, the play structure, the lawn, and even the old pond that still hadn't been filled in. What was different was not the park itself, but the way I saw the park.

We unloaded our car and made our way toward the lawn by the play structure. Our kids couldn't wait to explore this huge park and climb the play structure. But, before they ran away, I grabbed their hands and made us walk together, every step soaking in as much information as possible. I felt a little like a covert agent casing a room.

I noticed the obviously under-aged teens drinking beer and smoking pot in the gazebo at the other end of the lawn. With just a quick glance it was obvious that bathrooms were not clean, and the graffiti inside helped paint the picture of the additional recreational activities the bathrooms were used for. And the cement pond? Clearly a lawsuit waiting to happen.

I noticed some older elementary kids completely manhandling the play structure and daring each other to try more and more dangerous stunts off it. It seemed like there were a hundred kids running around with out any control or input from parents. How in the world were we supposed to keep track of our kids? And add to the mix an older man who didn't seem to have any kids with him at the park, but just sat on the bench watching and watching.

By the time we made it to our spot, I was a mess. What was supposed to be an afternoon at an amazing park became two hours of anxiety and high alert for me. What changed? Was the park always this dangerous and disgusting?

The more I've reflected on this experience, the more I realize that I'm the one who has changed. As a kid, I didn't have a care in the world. As a young adult, I was sure of my self and comfortable in my surroundings. Now, as a dad, I am responsible for two little lives, and I view the entire world through the lens of protective parent. And Pioneer Park, the place that was such a great place to be a kid, has become a huge ocean of potential death, danger and destruction.

Heightened Awareness of Danger is Important

For better or worse, we live in an age where we have been beaten over the head with all the potential dangers of the world we live in. Because of our news cycle and the internet, every awful thing that has happened anywhere in the world comes right into our homes and is told as if it's happening right outside the door. Besides the world news of fires, hurricanes, explosions, earthquakes, swine flu, bird flu, and killer bees, there are the kinds of crimes that terrify us parents and cause us to live in a constant state of fear.

These potential violent dangers seem to always be just below the surface. I feel it every time my son is out of my sight for even a second. I panic and scan the horizon for some perp who has run off with my kid. Throw into the mix allergies, food issues, and bee stings, and it seems like all day every day, I'm wading through one potentially dangerous situation after another.

When I talk to my mom about these sorts of fears she laughs, and tells stories of how my friends and I would spend hours running through the hills behind our house (while we were in elementary school). Even parents just ten years older don't seem to fully understand our anxiety. But when I get together with a group of parents with toddlers, it seems to be a fear we all share. I still don't get full weight of this fear and heightened awareness of potential danger. Every now and then I will forget how awful and dangerous the world is and will let my daughter go to the public bathroom by herself, only to be stopped with shrieks of horror by my wife and our friends.

This heightened awareness is part of our generation of parenting. There will be plenty of books written about it and the helpful, and harmful, side affects it brings. But my wife keeps insisting that three years old might not yet be the time to begin to let up. So, if this is our daily reality, maybe there is also a deeper spiritual reality that can be gleaned by our increased awareness to Stranger Danger.

Heightened Awareness of the Holy Spirit is the MOST Important

Living in our natural state of constant fear is not God's plan for our lives or our children's. But this heightened awareness we've developed means we can heighten our awareness of other things in our lives as well. In regards to our faith, we might be invited to raise our awareness of what God is doing in our lives and in the world around us. Maybe God is calling us into a heightened awareness of the Holy Spirit.

When we become Christians we receive the Holy Spirit as a seal, and are transformed into new creations. Often we don't feel like new creations because our external life has not fully conformed to our internal life. The biblical term for this is *sanctification*. It is the process of our entire lives transforming into our true identity as children of God. The number one way this comes about is by becoming more and more connected to the Holy Spirit.

In Romans chapter 8, the Apostle Paul writes about the contrast between a life lived in the flesh, and one lived in the Spirit. He says that the mind controlled by the Spirit has life and peace. (Romans 8:6) He goes on to say it is this Spirit which gives us power for life, confirms our identity as God's children, and will share in the love of God now and forever more. Amen!

This Holy Spirit at work in us is also at work in the world around us. Jesus confirms that His Father is always at work. His Holy Spirit is calling you and your kids to faith. He is directing His people to accomplish His purposes, and these include grace, mercy, forgiveness, reconciliation, and justice. The strange thing is that while God can do all of this by Himself, He actually chooses to allow us to partner with Him to accomplish these goals.

If we are listening, it is the Holy Spirit, the One who speaks in the still and quiet voice and invites us to be the very hands, feet, eyes, and ears of God. Because God gently invites us into these endeavors, we actually have to do some work to quiet our hearts and minds and learn how to discern the voice of God. This is not normal or natural to do in our day-to-day lives, but it is of utmost importance if we're going to be the people God desires us to be, and help our kids become the godly women and men that He has dreamed of them becoming.

We have gotten pretty good at developing a totally foreign awareness in our ability to discern Stranger Danger. We have done this because our children's physical safety is so important to us. And whatever is important to us we will put time and effort into achieving. The difficult thing is developing the longer perspective of awareness to discern what God is doing and wants to do in the lives of our kids. As we increase the importance of this awareness, we will gladly put in the increased time and effort to heighten our awareness of the Holy Spirit.

How Do You Do It?

Trying to describe the sense of awareness and anxiety that happens when we take our kids into a crowded space makes little sense to someone who doesn't have children. It doesn't mean that they can't learn to become more aware, it is just that it isn't important to them yet. This exact same reality is true regarding our heightened ability to discern the movement of the Holy Spirit. As it becomes more and more important to us personally and for the faith development of our kids, we will intentionally work it out.

The big question is, how do you actually *do* it? Just as our friend who doesn't have kids doesn't think about Stranger Danger, it isn't natural for us to hear and understand the Still Small Voice. Like anything, it is a process that takes time, effort and practice. Here are just a couple of simple exercises to develop our awareness.

Asking: The Holy Spirit is alive and is the One who offers life and peace. We do not have a dead faith or a distant God. It is an intimate relationship, and God invites us to ask, and promises that when we ask, we will receive, and when we knock, His door will be opened.

Tuning Your Ears: Just like those old-style radio dials, our ears have to be tuned toward the things of God. It takes effort and patience to turn the dial through all the static until you lock into the right station for music, news, or sports. Similarly, we must move through the static, working it out so we can hear from God. Jesus says that we are to "Pay close attention to what you hear. The closer you listen, the more understanding you will be given" (Mark 2:24).

Cleaning the Slate: Believe it or not, the ability to hear or not hear God also depends on our antenna. When we live in the flesh and have un-confessed sin in our lives, it corrodes our antenna and stifles our ability to hear from God and live into all that He has for us. Sin quenches the Holy Spirit, and the inverse is also true. A life that is sanctified and set apart increases connectivity in our antennas. There is no condemnation for those in Christ (another great nugget in Romans 8), so we can confess our sins freely, knowing that we are already accepted and forgiven--just in need of a cleaning.

Showing Up Where God is at Work: God is always at work, and it seems that when God's people gather, it is easier to notice what God is doing. Plus, if you miss it, there are others around to help guide you. There does seem to be a correlation, like the one in Acts 2 where God's people show up together to live life, pray, worship, eat, and share; and God shows up and making His presence known.

Write it Down: I've found that when I ask, God does actually show up. But if I'm not careful, I soon forget that truth and move on to the next crisis or drama. When we write it down, and document the ways God has shown up, we participate in the longest of biblical traditions, remembering. The entire Bible is an account of God's people remember His workings, and so our journals get to be our histories as well.

Questions for Reflection:

1) Reflect back on how you developed such a keen sense of Stranger Danger.
2) When was a time you felt like you had a heightened awareness to the Holy Spirit?
3) List out some of the things that were going on in your life that made you more aware.
4) Read Romans 8 and write up a compare and contrast list of life in the Spirit and life in the flesh.
5) What is something from the "How To" section that you can try out this week? Today?

chapter eight: SAY NO TO FACEBOOK: FASTING

Facebook Has Changed My Life

Have you sat down and actually kept track of what you do with your time? It is an awful exercise. It is awful because, if you do it honestly, you will probably come to the same conclusion I did: I waste an incredible amount of time. Think of how much time you spend surfing the web, checking Facebook, reading blogs, watching YouTube, sending emails, and waiting for the replies.

All the things that I think will help me accomplish more in a day actually detract from the things that are most important. The sad thing is I spend an incredible amount of time invested in the virtual me. Sad, because the virtual me often takes priority over the actual me.

Here is a fun experiment: Go to your local park--the place where parents go to play with their kids. Notice the parents, and notice the kids. The kids are all in, totally present in this moment playing at the park and enjoying time with their parents. The parents, on the other hand, are divided. They bounce their heads between their kids and their phones, checking in on the kids then sending a text or two, pushing the kids on the swing while reading emails, and then when the child does something

111

extraordinarily cute, out comes the phone and a picture is taken so the Facebook status can be updated.

Of all the ways I am present online, the one that has actually transformed my worldview is Facebook. What started out as a way to share pictures and funny things that happen throughout the day with my friends and family has taken on a life of its own. Sometimes I feel like something didn't really happen unless it gets documented in a posted picture or status update. I may be camping with my family, spending time with them, yet all the while I am compelled to check in on what my acquaintances are up to as I share with them pictures of my trip.

In and of itself this isn't that bad. But the fact is, I am with the most important people in the world to me, and while I should be present with them, my mind is racing, seeking something witty to share with my virtual community. All the while, my actual community wants to know why I love my phone more then them. The scariest thing is when my actual community could care less how much I am on my phone because they too are all on their phones working out their virtual selves at the cost of their actual selves.

Not only are my wife and I on our phones or computers working out this virtual reality, but when my kids interfere with me, I have set up games and websites for them to go and "interact" with. I'm telling myself that they are educational in purpose and it will even give my kids a leg up among their peers if they know how to use my laptop before they enter preschool. But what I am actually doing is teaching them to develop their virtual selves in place of their actual selves.

I get that we live in an era where the internet is vital to our lives. It has taken preeminence in the ways we communicate with friends, family, colleagues, and acquaintances. I am not saying that the sky is falling or that the internet is a bad thing. In fact I love the internet, and think that it's an amazing tool for just about everything! But if we aren't careful, the internet can become not just a gigantic time suck, but a true distraction from the real life, real relationships, and real things that God has called us to.

Going Old Skool: From Virtual to Actual

The virtual world is quite alluring in the way that it draws us in. I would think that most of us don't even consider we have a virtual reality. Those are for tech geeks, who get their news from Twitter, have a blog, and swap conspiracy theories with others in their pajamas. But when you consider Facebook as a blog, and look back on your browser history to see what information you consume and share, it becomes more and more apparent that there is a virtual you out there in cyber space, just as real as the real you reading this book right now.

Just as our actual life needs food and interaction to exist, our virtual life needs the same things. With out time or attention this life in cyberspace begins to atrophy and disappear. Think about what would happen if somehow the Facebook site shut down, for a day, a week, a month; or if one of your online communities ceased to exist. These mini versions of yourself would die along with the site. Because this hasn't happened, it's difficult to tell what sort of impact that would have on us. But I wonder.

While there isn't any hard evidence for this, I do think that the loss of virtual communities might actually enhance our actual communities. Both the virtual and actual person crave the same thing, to be known and to be significant. Being significant in a virtual world does have some benefit, but this benefit is only a shadow.

There is a blog I created and write on. As this blog gained in popularity, I became fixated on the number of hits I was receiving. On days my hit count was up, I felt important and valuable, but on days when I received little attention, I noticed myself questioning my worth. Yet who are these people that read my blog and what does it really matter to me in my actual life? Because I was tired of this emotional roller coaster I did some hard work and thought and prayed about why I cared so much. What I found was a bit alarming. All the work I did in my virtual life I did so I would feel valuable and significant in my actual life.

My virtual life is truly nothing apart from my actual life. It is my actual life that God has called me to live, it is my actual family God has called me to love, and it is my actual community God has called me to live with. These are people that I can't blow off until I feel like responding, like a text message. These are people who don't want to just listen to me pontificate about some subject the way I do on my blog. These are people who are not just interested in a cute picture and funny update like my Facebook friends. These are real people in real time who need me to be fully present.

The sad truth I have discovered is I have gotten swept up in my virtual life, and what makes it worse is that it's at the expense of my actual one. My spouse needs the actual me. My kids, for sure, need the actual me. Because I am a broken person, I am powerless to stop my addiction to my virtual life. Thankfully there are disciplines and practices that people of faith have been using for thousands of years as they strived to be completely present in their actual lives by mastering the distractions and hang-ups in their shadow lives.

The Tool God Uses: Fasting

Fasting is an ancient practice and one of the most effective of the traditional spiritual disciplines. When we take away something of value and importance, it heightens our awareness and senses. This happens in the physical world; people who have lost their sight may develop, for instance, an amazing ability to hear. This is also true in the spiritual world. When I fast from food I am reminded that my stomach and my physical and emotional desires are not the sum of who I am. I am more than my desires. My fulfillment and sustenance comes from God, not from the food I eat.

Another benefit of fasting is that it continually reminds us to reorient our thinking. When I fast from food I radically transform how I think throughout my day. I normally eat whenever I am hungry. Not eating when I am hungry does something in my brain, which now reminds me who really feeds me, or of a specific thing I might decide to pray for during this time of fasting. You would be surprised by how much you think about food when you fast from food, and this gives you an opportunity for God to transform you.

Fasting from food is the traditional version of fasting. Another version of fasting that I am currently observing and would encourage you to try is a fast from the Internet. I have been wrestling with this idea for a couple of months now, and am finally biting the bullet. And now, God has been slowly reorienting my heart, soul, and mind, to the point where I am looking forward to dying to my virtual life. To pull this off, I must turn off my shadow self, with the purpose and intention to develop my actual self.

At first this seems like an impossibility. I recently took some high school students on a mission trip to Guatemala, and watched the unbelievable fruit that began to grow when they simply unplugged for a week. I watched distant and apathetic individual students transform into a genuine community who were present and could actually care for each other and the community we were serving. Being present allowed them to fully engage in real life and real ministry. They built new friendships, had to work through conflict, lengthened their attentions span, and even connected with God in new and deep ways.

By turning off the internet, I am looking forward to being present. I'm tired of being tethered to a world that has little-to-no bearing on my real life. My real life is here in flesh and blood, with my friends and family. My real life is with my children and in pouring all of who I am into them. It would be a crime if I could not engage them because I'm thinking about things and people who surely are not thinking about me in the slightest. I definitely don't want to communicate that the false reality of my virtual world is more important to them. Or worse, I would hate to already train them to be developing their virtual life at the expense of their actual life.

By turning off the Internet, I am looking forward to contributing to my family, my friends and to the world. Consuming all that information online has a way of tricking us into thinking we are participating in some grand conversation. The truth is that we are just consuming, and affirming the consumption of others. By turning this off for a while, I will be forced to take a break from consuming, from wasting time, from being inefficient, and from not being present. Without the distraction of the Internet, I hope I will be able to bring something that is real and of value to the table.

Giving up the Internet will force me to grow up and mature as well. Whenever the conversation grows stale or I have some time to kill, I have traditionally used that as a cue to go online and check Facebook or read a blog. Now, I will have to re-learn how to have conversation, how to ask questions, how to share my life. I have to show up and contribute.

The Internet is not a bad thing; in fact it is a great tool and resource. I've just noticed that I (and I suspect you as well), have transitioned from being fully present as I invest in my kids, friends and family, to participating in this weird form of idol worship known as consuming information for the sake of consuming it. For me, I've been reminded that my real life is with the flesh and bones of the people in my proximity, and that they need me to be more present than I have been in a long while. For me to grow in the ways I need to grow in my walk with God, I must have more mental space to be quiet and listen and not fill it with nonsense from online.

For these reasons, I am accepting this invitation from God to mix up my virtual diet, for the purpose of personal and spiritual growth. I am trusting that God will use this dramatic increase in spare time to connect with my family, to love on my kids, and to actually be present in conversations. I am trusting that God will use this free space in my mind to prune the dead and dying things and cause new growth, to actually allow God to search me, know me, test me, reveal any offensive ways in me, and direct me along the path to everlasting life.

Questions for Reflection:
1) Count how much time you spend online, on your phone, on Facebook in a day.
2) How much of that time is while you are with your children?
3) What about your virtual life is so important to you?
4) How has your virtual life taken preeminence over your actual life?
5) Would you consider an Internet fast? Technology fast?

chapter nine: SCRAPBOOKING:
THE OLDEST OF SPIRITUAL DISCIPLINES

The Joys of Die Cuts and Stamps

Sometimes I can just get lost in the world of scrapbooking. I recently went onto scrapbook.com and was immediately drawn to "Jill's Deals." Who is this Jill person and why does she get prominence on this website? Because I love a good deal, I immediately clicked the button and was taken just as immediately to the sale section. This section had everything a scrapbooker would ever need: binding tools, distressing tools, paper, ribbon, totes, and just about every type of cutting system ever invented, and all for 30% - 50% off!

OK, I have to admit it, I actually never get lost in the world of scrapbooking. In fact whenever I find myself in a craft store (which is rarely), I look down the scrapbooking isles and am feel immediately overwhelmed. While it is true that I don't know the first thing about scrapbooking, it is a craft/art form I respect. The time and effort put into creating a book that tells a wonderful story about a baby's birth, a couple's engagement, a celebration of friendship, or the highlights of a year is a meaningful gift that continues to be a blessing for years after.

While some people are satisfied with just having some pictures on their computers to share with friends and family, those with more time and passion take the best of those photos and actually print them out. But for the select few, there are those who take this passion to a completely different level. These people are ***scrapbookers***.

Scrapbookers enjoy life, are passionate about the people they share life with, and have found a medium through which to express this joy and share it with others. It is amazing to me that there is an entire industry devoted to this craft, devoted to nurturing friendships and celebrating memories. At best, I might print off a picture and send it as a postcard to a friend. But a scrap-booker, armed with the Crop-A-Dile II, fancy paper, and several dye cutting systems, would take that same picture and create a postcard that would get put in a place of honor and would build strong heart strands between the scrap-booker and the person who received, not just a postcard, but a gift.

I don't know if there is a scientific study out there on this, but I would be willing to bet that scrap-bookers probably enjoy a sunnier worldview than the rest of us, who simply take and look at pictures on our phones. While I wait for the study to be done on this, I have enough anecdotal evidence to supports my hypothesis. My theory is that scrapbookers simply rehearse a positive worldview. Their entire hobby is centered around taking the pictures that capture the best of life and present the pictures in a way that is compelling and worthy of display. And these displays are seen so often that these become the dominant memories of that household.

Grumbling Actually Impacts Our World View

It takes a significant amount of work to train our brains to remember the best of life and to have a long enough catalogue of these memories to shape our worldview. Unfortunately, the opposite is also true. By putting no effort into our memories, our brains become cloudy with the common and mundane, and punctuated with memories of pain and heartbreak.

See if this is true in your own life. Take a piece of paper and on one column list the 10 best things that have happened this year and in the other, list the 10 worst. For me, my worst column will fill up the fastest. Because I don't want to seem unhappy I would stop at 5 or 6 and then intentionally fill out the good side before going back to the bad. But the truth is, my painful and hurtful memories are much more prominent in my memory then my happy and pleasant ones.

I have a friend who seems to be naturally pessimistic. He is convinced that he was born with a black cloud over his head. Because this is his worldview, everything that happens in his life either builds on this presupposition and solidifies his worldview, or goes against it and is quickly forgotten. Someone taking his parking space at work, catching the flu for the second time this season, breaking his arm snowboarding, roof leaking, kid getting put on the worst soccer team and not getting in the same class as his friends; these all add to his idea that the world is against him and provide more examples that he's drawn the short end of the stick.

The fact that he has a great job that pays for his home seems to elude him. Of course the roof is leaking; it's an older house and we had the wettest winter on record last year. But every one of these negative memories darkens the lines in his brain, convincing him he was actually born under a dark cloud. And in this process, he forgets easily the many blessings in his life, both material and relational.

Grumbling and complaining has this way of limiting our memory. Sometimes in the summer it will get to be so hot that there seems to be no way to cool down. I will find myself leaving my office to get into my car that is blistering hot, only to get home to a house that feels like a sauna, which makes my entire family irritable and snappy. All we do is sit around in the heat and complain about how awful it is, and before we know it we are down this road of it being the hottest summer on record and wishing it was some other season. But we have this exact conversation in the dead of winter as well. Come to think of it, we have this conversation any time the weather doesn't conform to our plans.

With a limited memory we have no ability to remember the natural rhythms of life. Having little memory of these natural rhythms is mostly annoying and makes me grumpy. Of course it is going to be hot in summer and cold in winter! The scary thing is how grumbling seems to actually cloud our memories of the more important things in life surrounding our relationships, and impacts the most important memories regarding the faithfulness of God.

The Oldest Discipline: Remembering God's Goodness

All of scripture is one giant story of God's faithfulness to His people. God called Abraham to be the father of a special people who would were vital for His redemptive plan for the entire planet. He gave Abraham specific promises; he would be given a specific piece of land, he would become a great nation, would make his name great, and all the people of the earth would be blessed through him.

It is this promise that began to shape the family story of the Israelites. This promise of a family that would outnumber the stars and were a special portion to the God Most High built an identity that has never wavered. When God's people went to escape the famine and moved to Egypt as a favored family, they had no idea that this would turn into one of the darkest chapters of their story. This prominent family became a threat to Pharaoh and ended up as slaves for over 400 years.

In dramatic fashion God came up with a plan to rescue His people from slavery and bring them to the Promised Land; the land flowing with milk and honey, the land promised to their patriarch, Abraham. After the plagues, after the crossing of the Red Sea, after the miraculous provision of water, manna and quail, God made a covenant with His people, and gave Moses the ten commandments on Mount Sinai. The beginning of the law starts with a call to remember God's goodness and faithfulness. "I am the Lord your God, who brought you out of Egypt, out of the land of slavery." (Exodus 20:2)

This Exodus story is the pinnacle of God's faithfulness to His people. He dramatically revealed His power in the miracles preformed and the needs provided for. And what is even more important is God proved He would keep His word. He promised a land and a kingdom to His servant Abraham, and fulfilled His promise when the

Israelites followed Joshua in taking back the Promised Land.

From Exodus 20 through the rest of scripture, New and Old Testaments, we find a continued call to His people to remember this story, to remember the ways that God has always comes through for His people, the way that God rescues us from slavery and delivers us to the Promised Land. I am amazed that, to this day, there are people all over the world who identify themselves as decedents of Abraham, Isaac, and Jacob, and who remember the ways God has been faithful to His people, and long for Him to be faithful again.

Jesus continued the tradition and discipline of remembering God's faithfulness and plan when He celebrated the Passover dinner with His disciples. The most important meal eaten in the Jewish calendar, the Passover Seder is the meal that commemorates the story of God rescuing His people. It was celebrated every year after the actual Passover and is still celebrated today.

It was at this meal that Jesus added fuller meaning to the elements of the dinner--identifying Himself as the Passover Lamb who would take the punishment of death so death could "pass over" His people. He took the unleavened bread and broke it, symbolizing His body that would be broken for us, then took the wine and declared a New Covenant sealed in His blood, blood to be shed for our sins. No longer were we to be people under the law, but instead, people born of the Spirit. And we were told that we are to celebrate this Passover meal, the Lord's Supper, Communion, the Eucharist, in remembrance of Him. And as often as we eat the bread and drink from the cup we remember and proclaim His death and resurrection, and anticipate His return.

Remembering the ways that God has shown up is vital to our faith. The biggest ways we see that are through the Exodus and the Lord's Supper. These two stories are encompassing enough to include all people from all time. It is through the Lord's Supper we see that the promise God made to Abraham has been fulfilled completely, and truly all people on the earth have been blessed through his line.

But it is not just in the big story that God shows up. God shows up every day in the big *and* little things. He answers prayer, comforts our hearts, and directs our path. He is active and alive. And if we are going to live into all that God has for us, then we have to develop some sort of mechanism to remember the times when God does actually show up. We do it through Communion to remind the large church of God's faithfulness, now we must do it personally within our own families.

Reshaping Our Story

This is where scrapbookers have a great head start. They have a built-in mechanism for shaping memories, instilling them into their worldview, and passing them on to others. While this is important to do with our general memories and within our friendships, we must do this with our faith and the development of our faith story specifically and intentionally.

We often are too comfortable in our posture of grumbling that we miss out and easily forget all the ways that God has been faithful to us and to our family. Sure, there have been and will be awful trials and dark times. I am not saying that we are to cover up or ignore hardship and pain, but I am definitely saying that we are to develop a story that is full and grand--a story that is shaped by God's goodness, where heartache and pain are allowed to exist, and are anticipated to be redeemed, in huge and amazing ways.

We need to have a way to stop and remember the places where God showed up and answered prayer, pouring out His love and grace, so that they don't just get washed away with other more common memories. When I was a camp counselor we called these times watermarks. You know when you drive by a lake and you can see along the shore and sometimes along the cliffs high places where the water has once reached and has left a mark, a reminder to all who see how high the water has been? In the same way, we need to have watermarks in our lives that remind us, our families, and all who pass by, that God has shown up at a specific time and place and is to be remembered and celebrated.

I document these watermarks in my journal. They're also documented in items around our house that remind me of places and times God have shown up. These watermarks have become part of our family story. We have gotten in the habit of crafting a family story that is elevated from the logistics of the day and celebration or grief of events, but instead are framed in the context of the Exodus or the Lord's Supper. We are a people group, a family that is sometimes in slavery, sometimes in the desert, and sometimes in the Promised Land. We are a people who have been rescued from sin and death and are invited into a New Covenant full of life and power from the Holy Spirit.

The memories we choose to dwell on are the ones that shape our story and worldview. Scrapbookers get this. As people of God, may we continue to develop a family story that fits within the greater story of God!

Questions For Reflection:
1) Make the suggested list of 10 good and 10 bad memories of this last year.
2) Would you say you are pessimistic or optimistic? What stories do you use to inform this worldview?
3) List out 5-10 watermarks where God has shown up for you and your family.
4) What are things you do to remember these times and places better?
5) How can you place your family story within God's story?

chapter ten: BEDTIME: RESHAPING THE DAY

The Most Wonderful Time of the Day

There is something almost magical about the end of the day. We have spent the entire day with our kids, or at work, and we are tired and need to veg out. The problem is, having little kids completely destroys any chance of disengaging and winding down. For this reason, we have implemented a strict 7:00 bedtime. By 7:00 our kids are wiped out and, even if they aren't, I am!

As we sit down for dinner and enjoy conversation, master the art of using silverware, and notice all of the additional cleanup that will have to take place as food seems to get everywhere, I find myself daydreaming about 7:30, the most wonderful time of the day. It is the time that marks the end of a long day full of joy and chaos, and begins the time of rest and restoration for me and for my wife and I as a couple. By 7:30, the kids are in bed (most of the time), the kitchen has been cleaned up, and the house put back together. It is time to pour a glass of wine, sit on the couch, and decompress.

But before we can get to 7:30, there are some very important steps that have to happen between dinner and couch time. What I have found is that this last hour of the day for our kids has proven to actually be the most important hour in determining how the rest of the night would unfold. It is the hour where we help them wind down from the day, pour love and affection on them, and intentionally walk with them as they begin their own walk with God.

A Calming Rhythm

Every family has different needs and different personalities. For our family, we have found that creating a sacred rhythm for the last hour of the day has been invaluable for their emotional, physical, and spiritual development. Of course there are always things that come up and changes have to happen, but for the most part, five out of seven nights look pretty much identical.

After dinner we send our kids to the bath. Bath time has got to be the best thing ever invented. For 20 minutes or so, they soak in the tub, play with toys, and relax in a warm and contained space. All of the grime and food they have collected on their person throughout the day gets washed away, and by the time they get out, they are once again the clean and precious babies you remember them to be.

Once the bath is done, we conclude our evening hygiene with pajamas, teeth brushing, and hair brushing. Right before our eyes our wild toddlers have transitioned in to calm and clean babies, ready to be hugged and kissed and hugged some more. So that is exactly what we do.

We head out to the couch with my daughter or the bed for my son and cuddle up as we read stories. Some of these stories are fun and silly, but we try to bring in at least one bible story a night. You might not think it matters at this age, but I am impressed with the biblical knowledge that my kids have already gained by simply reading colorful and cartoonish bible stories over and over again.

After stories, it's time for the final lap. With some time for reflecting on the day and prayer time left, couch time for the wife and me is just around the corner. If I'm not careful, I can actually miss the most important part of the nightly routine while anticipating my own time to unwind. I have to make a mental choice to die to that desire for a few more minutes, because this last step is the most important one of the night.

The Need for Daily Reflection

Without reflection, we become people who simply move through life reacting to every circumstance that comes our way. Reflection gives us the ability to process what has happened and what is happening, consider the state of these circumstances currently, and might possibly in the future impact us, and then make choices accordingly. By reflecting, we move from reacting to responding, the bread and butter of the Christian faith.

The apostle John writes that, "We love because he first loved us." (1 John 4:9) Jesus loves us and has proven it over and over and over. But in order to receive this love, in order to have this love actually impact us and transform us, we have to stop and reflect. "Jesus loves me this I know, for the Bible tells me so" is a great song with a powerful message. But usually we sing it with our kids not really thinking about what this song is all about.

In order to fully embrace the love of God, we must make personal reflection part of our diet. And if our kids are going to embrace the love of God, we have to help model what this actually looks like.

The mystics called this sort of prayer the Examen of Consciousness. This means developing our ability to reflect and take inventory of our day. We reflect back on the places where we saw God show up, the places where God probably did show up but we missed it in the moment, the places we partnered with God in His values and purposes, and the times in the day when our selfishness, pride and rebellion got the better of us.

When we do this sort of reflection we train our hearts and minds to be more aware of the things of God and the movement of God in our actual daily lives. For me, I often find there are more times in the day I miss it than when I partner with God. But by reflection on these moments, I train my brain to become more aware, and sure enough I start to notice them in the moment rather than only upon reflection. When I notice them in the moment, I have the opportunity to respond right then and there. The more I reflect, the more I can respond, and the more I respond, the more I actually fall in love with God and allow His love to transform me.

This prayer of consciousness is difficult and takes work. But this challenge has amazing results. My biggest prayer for my kids, apart from them knowing and loving God, is for them to be reflective people. I want to help them develop the ability to not just react to the circumstances in their lives, to simply choose the easiest, short term, solution to the problem. Reflection is the only way that they will be able to respond to the world around them, to gain knowledge and wisdom so they will know how to have lives that are marked more by partnering with the purposes of God, rather than lives of selfishness and rebellion.

To do this with a toddler is actually easier than it seems. Once the books are read and they are tucked into bed, we have the opportunity to have them reflect on their day. By simply asking them what was the best part of their day, we get to help shape the story of their day with God as the hero, pouring out His love and blessing on them. When we ask them to reflect on the worst part of their day, this usually provides an opportunity to reflect on conflict or them not getting their way. Usually some sort of sin and selfishness surrounded that incident. This is a perfect segue into showing how God's story of love and forgiveness actually impacts their little story and takes them into the bigger story. Because of Jesus' love for us, we are forgiven and get a fresh start.

The best part about helping our kids reflect on the best and worst part of the day is that we are helping them develop a worldview where God is in the center and gets to be thanked for His numerous blessings. We also help our kids unload the sin and garbage in their lives. We forget, but a little life that is full of conflict and rebellion is like a little backpack filling up with rocks. This pack gets unbearably heavy for them, and actually impacts their character. By giving them tools to reflect on these things and a way to unload their personal backpacks we are creating opportunities for the Holy Spirit to grab hold of their hearts, and plant the seed of faith, in good and fertile soil.

A Simple Prayer

When we have walked through the bedtime rhythm, the time has come to wrap up our time in prayer. Because this prayer time is with toddlers, there needs to be a lot of latitude given regarding the seriousness and reverence that is held to. The bedtime prayer is about setting up rhythms and patterns for continued conversation with God and reflection on His working in our lives.

Our family has developed a prayer time that ranges from serious to silly. Over the course of a week we try to touch on different themes in our prayers. This prayer time has become distinct from the discipline of grace before a meal. For whatever reason, grace has already become a rote prayer that is almost identical from meal to meal.

Our evening prayers are our opportunity to actually model prayer and our own faith with God to our kids as they begin to walk with God. We alternate with who goes first and when it is my turn to pray I have to pause and make sure that I am actually praying, not just teaching. If I can actually make my prayers genuine and heartfelt, they do more teaching then my "teaching" prayers could ever do.

The prayers we say with our kids have three parts. The first part is thanking God for the day and the blessings we have experienced throughout it. This is easy and natural. We simply start with the prompt, "Dear Jesus, today I am thankful for ... "

The second part of our prayer is the part we rotate throughout the week. We want to help our kids develop a view of prayer that is more relational and interactive. We have decided to make adoration, confession, and prayer requests part of our prayer diet. Because toddlers have a limited attention span and limited vocabulary, we walk through these concepts and model them in our own prayers.

Adoration is a big word and makes little sense for toddlers. But the truth is that God, just in His nature alone, deserves to be worshiped and adored. To help our kids develop this, we give them another simple prompt. "Dear Jesus, some of the things I love about You are..."

Confession is a little more difficult. However, on the nights where we spend some real time reflecting on our day, we often come across an instance or two where our kids have screwed up and have done something wrong, rude, or mean. I always have plenty of examples of losing my cool and being short, or not listening. After we have reflected on these places we have been wrong and have sinned, we get the opportunity to talk about how Jesus forgives us our sins when we confess them, or tell them to God and ask for Him to forgive us. The prompt we use is, "Dear Jesus, please forgive me for..."

Because we want our kids to know that God loves them and cares about their lives and actually interacts with them, we make sure that part of our prayer time is spent sharing prayer requests. It is really a fun experience to ask our kids what they would like to pray for, or who they would like to pray for. When we are really on our A-game we also write these down and occasionally go back to show them how God shows up and hears our prayers. For this part our prompt is, "Dear Jesus, tonight I would like to pray for..."

After we have started with a prayer of thanksgiving, and then have picked one of the three other types of prayers, it will be my turn to pray. Like I mentioned before, it is important that these actually be my prayers too, not just a teaching exercise. After my daughter and I have both prayed, we do the Lord's Prayer together.

This is an important prayer and an easy win. By ending the same way every night, we have developed a liturgy that caps our nightly rhythm. These rhythms bring comfort and safety to our developing kids as well as cultivating good soil for God to plant in. Because the Lord's Prayer is long and complicated, I have found ways to gradually mix it up and even make it fun.

Until they have learned the entire thing, which actually only takes a couple of weeks or so, I start each sentence and pause for them to complete it by saying the last word.

Our _____,
Which art in _____,
Hallowed be your _____.
Thy Kingdom _____,
Thy will be _____,
On earth as it is in _____.
Give us _____,
Our daily _____.
And forgive us our _____,
As we forgive those who have sinned against _____.
And lead us not into _____,
But deliver us from _____.
For Thine is the _____, the _____, and the gloryE
Forever and ever and ever and ever and ever and ever!
(Kiss good night)

Good night!

Questions for Reflection:
1) Have you reflected on a bedtime rhythm that communicates your family's values and worldview?
2) When you reflect on the rhythms of your family are there places where you are simply reacting to circumstances and are being blown around like a ship without a rudder?
3) Give the Examen of Consciousness prayer a try. Spend 15 minutes and write down the places in your day where you saw God at work, where you missed God being at work, where you partnered with God in his values and purposes, and the parts where sin and selfishness crept in.
4) What do your bedtime prayers communicate about your view of God? What should you keep and what should you add or change?

chapter eleven: MIDNIGHT MAYHEM:
THOUGH I WALK THROUGH THE
VALLEY, YOU ARE WITH ME

When Am I at My Worst: 2:00 AM!

For whatever reason, the hours between 7:00 PM and 7:00 AM bring all sorts of chaos and crisis to our family. From the day our first child was born, nighttime has been the absolute worst in our home.

OK, maybe it wasn't the *very* first day, but within two weeks of our son being born, we realized that his sleep patterns were exactly opposite from the rest of civilized society—and ours. He slept all day and was beautiful and perfect for our friends and family, but like a vampire, as soon as the sun came down, he woke up and was ready to party. We tried everything we could think of to get his sleeping habits under control. I am sad to say that there was nothing we did that worked. But in a matter of weeks we seemed to at least have this problem under some sort of control.

Control is such a funny word when it comes to little babies. And whatever sense of control we thought we had was quickly taken away as he developed and awful case of acid reflux. For whatever reason, it was only after his nighttime feeding. His dinner upset his stomach so much that he would scream for hours, stopping only when he was too tired to cry anymore.

After six solid months without a full night of sleep, I was at the end of my rope. It was time for research. I think I read just about every book on the subject and talked with doctors, family and friends. Everyone had their own pet solutions they claimed were the only true way to help your kid sleep through the night. Sure enough after all the research, we did find one plan that worked. And what we found is every baby seems to respond to a different program. When your baby responds to one program, you become a "true believer" in that program. But this is less about the program and more about your baby.

Just as our son was starting to sleep through the night, we decided it was time to put him in his own room. This decision disrupted his new rhythm, and brought with it never-ending options for midnight mayhem. He would wake up hungry, from a nightmare, or just wake up, and therefore had to communicate to me and our entire house by screaming his guts out.

And then we brought our daughter into the world. Just as we were on the verge of getting our son to sleep through the night, we started the whole process over from scratch. What worked with one child was an anathema to the other.

Between our two kids, we've experienced years without a full night of sleep. We have experienced the embarrassment of our kids waking up our friends when we visited on vacation and bringing in the morning a couple hours early for an entire campground. We experienced middle of the night bedwetting and laundry, including our own bed. And unfortunately we have experienced my awful reactions to the compounding sleep deprivation. In the middle of the night, when my kids are crying and at their neediest because something is not right, I have found that I am least emotionally available to care for them.

I need my sleep, and without it, I have no patience. It is in the dark of the night that my true character is revealed and how I walk through it sets up patterns for future success or destruction between my kids and me.

Dark Night of the Soul

A few years ago my wife and I were having dinner with some family friends. They are a few years older than we are, and significantly further down the road when it comes to their faith and walk with God. As we were having dinner, this family friend began sharing about a recent season in her walk with Jesus.

Being that she is such a woman of deep faith and integrity, I perked up when she referred to this last season as the Dark Night of the Soul. This term made this last leg of her journey with God sound both awful and poetic.

She went on to describe the last year or so as a time where, for whatever reason, her prayer life felt like a desert and God was a million miles away, if there at all. For en entire year, every spiritual exercise she did brought with it absolutely zero experiential benefit.

Now, I have been through periods where my own sin and rebelliousness has made it feel like God was distant. These were times where I clearly wanted to go in my own direction and was not that keen on what sort of things God had for me, and sure enough, the further I walked away from God, the further He felt. But this Dark Night of the Soul sounded completely different.

This seeming abandonment by Jesus to one of the most faithful saints I know didn't seem to make sense in my understanding of faith and how it all works. If you put in good effort, Jesus meets you and communes with you. I even mentioned it earlier: ask and it will be given, knock and the door is opened. But this is the problem when we only take a few of our favorite passages of scripture and develop a faith just around them.

Jesus, who for sure knew no rebellion or sin, experienced this when He was dying on the cross. He quotes the famous prayer found in Psalm 22, "My God, My God, why have You forsaken me?" (Matthew 27:46 and Psalm 22:2) It is this prayer that my friend identified with, and, she continued sharing, found that many other amazing Christians and prayer warriors have experienced as well.

I discovered that the term "Dark Night of the Soul" has been around for quite some time. A Catholic mystic named Saint John of the Cross wrote a poem about this in the 16th Century. After his poem, he then wrote an incredibly deep (and hard to understand!) commentary of his own poem.

This entire idea of the Dark Night, a season of prayer where one feels isolated and abandoned, during the very act in which one is supposed to feel intimate with God, fascinated me. I decided to read up on this whole concept, and figured the best place to go was to the man who started it all, Saint John. But wading through a poem and commentary from the 16th century is as difficult as you would think, and more difficult than I thought. Thankfully, the good people at Wikipedia have offered up a very succinct and understandable conclusion.

Wikipedia highlights that for all the difficulties found during this period, it brings with it some amazing benefits.

Rather than resulting in permanent devastation, the Dark Night is regarded by mystics and others as a blessing in disguise, whereby the individual is stripped (in the dark night of the senses) of the spiritual ecstasy associated with acts of virtue. Although the individual may for a time seem to outwardly decline in his or her practices of virtue, in reality he becomes more virtuous, as she is being virtuous less for the spiritual rewards (ecstasies in the cases of the first night) obtained and more out of a true love for God. It is this purgatory, a purgation of the soul, that brings purity and union with God.

How one handles this time of darkness is key. I think my inclination was to start drifting and become disillusioned if my walk with God became as described above, especially if it wasn't for any blatant sin or rebellion on my part. But if we have the character to push through these dark nights in our faith, then there are spiritual rewards and richness on the other side. It seems like every more mature Christian has experienced some season like this, and those who have remained faithful till the dawn all attest to the depth of blessing God has for them on the other side.

If this Dark Night of the Soul has spiritual benefit to those who continue to walk through dark and lonely valleys as they work out their faith, I think there must be parallels for the Long and Dark Night of Little Kids. This time of one, two, three, or even more years where we are sleep deprived might actually be a spiritual blessing for us as well. As we walk through every night with dread and discomfort waiting for the mayhem to ensue, God desires to meet us in this season, refine our character, and actually purify our union with Him and with our children.

Darkest Just Before the Dawn

As a general rule, I hate clichés and refuse to use them. So, I apologize for slapping a bumper sticker on one of the hardest aspects of raising toddlers. There are few things more infuriating than when I share about something difficult I'm walking through to only have the person across the table from me hand me a bumper sticker. It reminds me of the passage in James when he lays out the people who, seeing someone in need, as religious people, offer up a blessing and walk away.

A cliché is like that. There is no engagement, no empathy, and barely even sympathy. Unfortunately, clichés are clichés because they simply and quickly communicate a very true point. And this reality shouldn't be missed, just because it comes in the form of a bumper sticker.

The sleepless nights that surround the first several years of a child's life can be nerve-wracking. And for all the poor choices and reactions that accompany those of us parents who have been sleep deprived for years, this cliché is an important bumper sticker that we must get our heads around: *It is always the darkest just before the dawn.*

If you have ever been camping or even slept outside, with the wrong sleeping bag you will notice this strange phenomenon, just before the sun comes up the temperature drops, the dew shows up in force, and what was a nice night of camping enjoying the stars turns out being a night being soaked and cold.

For as long as I can remember, every day has consisted of two parts, daytime and then nighttime. Without fail nighttime always ends and sure enough the sun does actually begin to rise and with it brings a new day accompanied by new mercies. But the moments before the sunrises are the darkest and coldest.

It is vital to remember that these sleepless nights and the heightened stress and anxiety are only for a relatively short season. And sure enough, one day it will all be over, and just as soon as it started, it will end. The kids will sleep through the night, stop wetting the bed, and quit being a nuisance to our family, friends and neighbors who have unfortunately decided to spend the night in our vicinity. Pretty soon they will learn how to work the TV and enjoy cartoons on Saturdays, and before we know it, we won't be able to even get them out of bed before noon at all.

Best Words Of Wisdom Regarding Midnight Mayhem

Simply knowing that these sleepless nights are a temporary and that they often resemble the Dark Night of the Soul, (or even the valley of the Shadow of Death), still isn't the most helpful for those who find themselves in the darkest hour of the night.

As I've said, as someone who values my sleep, those sleepless nights haven't brought out the best in me. At

2:00 AM my fuse is non-existent and the frustration, harsh words, evil looks, and stomping my feet are at their worst. Holding a screaming baby, listening to a toddler scream herself to sleep, or trying to convince my preschooler to stay in their own bed seems to always go poorly in the darkest part of the night.

Not long ago, my wife had a brilliant idea for a strategy to deal with these sleepless nights. Maybe we should cherish this season, this short time of our lives where our kids want to be close to us and need our care and comfort and embrace it.

I know there are tons of books with all sorts of different strategies on dealing with these sleepless nights. I know, because I discovered all of them when I did my original research. Some of these are great but would never work in our family. I am positive you have read one or two or ten of these books also. I am not advocating a certain philosophy regarding sleep habits or boundaries on the family bed, I am simply identifying that no one book can give solutions to the multi-faceted dynamics at work with all the baggage and different personalities found in an individual nuclear family.

What my wife brought to my attention is that the book we decided to follow, which worked well for one child, didn't work at all for the other. And instead of making our children conform, maybe we could embrace this time and reexamine what our kids need most from us. And the answers came in the most unexpected places.

There is a midweek bible study my wife participates in with women from our church who are all different ages. One week, one of these mothers shared how her heart

144

was just broken because her teenage son seems to be always upset with her and doesn't want anything to do with her. He hasn't said one nice thing in months and she couldn't even remember the last time he even hugged her. (Adolescence will for sure be another Dark Night of parenting, but that is another book.) This conversation prompted my wife and I to have a conversation about how the time will be here before we know it that our kids will want nothing to do with us. So for this very short season, we have decided to soak up as much cuddling and loving on our kids as they can take.

The way we decide to walk through this Dark Night sets up patterns in our families and with our kids. It sets up patterns in our faith and defines our character. When we remain faithful, our character is refined and our relationships remain intact. If we pull the ejection handle too soon, either on our kids or on our faith, we will miss out on the most beautiful part of every day, the dawn.

Questions for Reflection:
1) Has there been a season in your faith that felt like the Dark Night of the Soul? How did you handle it? What did you learn from it?
2) What are your bedtime rules? How did they come to be? Are they best for each child and for where they are developmentally?
3) Who are some friends who are just a little bit further down the road from this period of life you can find support and encouragement from?
4) You should go and hug on your kids right now! Before you know it, they won't let us near them.

chapter twelve: I WILL NEVER...
A LIFETIME OF TEACHABIITY

A Unique Perspective

Long before I took on the title of father, I walked alongside other fathers and mothers as their children journeyed through the joys and destruction of adolescence. I have been working with students and their parents for over 15 years, and during this time I have seen firsthand the amount of carnage that can happen during a very short time span.

In the real world, these parents were high-powered professionals and well-respected in their circle of friends. But in my office they were tentative and insecure. For what parent of a teenager feels comfortable walking into their Youth Pastor's office to walk through the latest spat of chaos within their child's life?

A couple of years ago I met with a father after church regarding his teenaged daughter. I have only known this man at church, in his casual wear. This late 40's father loved his Tommy Bahama shirts, and honestly I always just thought of him as a little goofy and even insecure. The truth was, this wasn't the first time we met regarding his daughter.

The first time we met it was about his daughter's spiraling grades. Then the conversations moved to her stubbornness and disrespectfulness at home, and this last meeting was going to be difficult because it was about her bad-boy boyfriend. He was heartbroken and gentle as he spoke of his disappointment with his daughter and of himself. We were mourning the dream he had for his little angel, a dream that seemed to be ruined with little possibility of redemption. It was a difficult conversation, followed by more difficult ones.

The reason I bring up this dad and his Tommy Bahama shirts is because the only context through which I really know this dad is the exposed prism of his family chaos. My entire view of him changed when he invited me to have lunch one day, a day we had to meet at his office. I got there early, only to see this dad be, not goofy or passive in the slightest, but as a powerful and respected CFO of a large corporation. And while we were trying to enjoy a little small talk on our way to lunch, people regarding enormous projects worth millions of dollars kept stopping him. To tell you the truth, it was a little overwhelming, and it put me in my place.

Although this dad is at the top of his game professionally, he realizes that he has a long way to go in being the parent God desired him to be and become. He no longer treats his family like his employees as he bosses them around and marks out a clear and logical plan with measurable goals. His family is much more fluid than a business, and parenting a teenaged daughter is about as fluid as it gets. This dad has finally come to realize that his best laid plans for his family, for his daughter, have been severely uprooted, and he must now eat some crow as he develops a new plan forward that is less fixed in stone and more fixed in the presence of God.

I can't tell you the number of parents, who, though know-it-alls during their child's preschool and early elementary school years, have started to disappear from our church community. If you present your family as people who have it all together and have a plan that is unwavering (you would even call it full of purpose and intention), then when the chaos begins, there are often too many self-induced obstacles in the way of leaning into community, asking for help, and inviting others and God to walk through these years with you.

Because I have been privileged to see parenting on the back-end first, there seems to be one thing the parents who survive into and past their children's teen aged years have in common: they never say never.

Never Say Never!

This phrase is so much more than a great James Bond film or a popular Justin Bieber song. It is actually a posture, an approach to life and all the decisions that have to be made. It has to do with decisions that are to be made currently and most important, decisions that will need to be made in the future.

Unlike parents of teenagers, parents of toddlers and preschoolers are the most confident and self-assured-appearing people I have come in contact with. I can't tell you how many conversations I have been a part of where I have listened to new parents lay out their entire lives with all the conviction in the world as they outlined their parenting philosophy, discipline strategy, and scholastic career of their child. The most common phrase in these circles seems to be, "I will never . . . "

I will never let my child sleep in our bed.

I will never spank my child.

I will never have a child who is messy in public.

I will never let my child suck their thumb.

I will never allow my child to use a bottle after age 2.

I will never let my child drink anything other than breast milk.

I will never let my child throw a temper tantrum in public.

I will never send my child to daycare. (Why would I pay for someone else to raise my child?)

I will never send my child to public school.

I will never let sports get in the way of our church life or family vacations.

I will never _____.

In every circle of friends there are plenty of examples to choose from, examples of parents who know exactly what they will and will not allow in the raising of their children. Truthfully, these parents intimidate me. It is like playing the "God told me" card. There is no discussion and their confidence is their argument.

Don't get me wrong; I think parenting with intention, having a plan, is a very good thing. I also think that trying to be sensitive to the Holy Spirit and go in the direction He is leading is the highest aim. But there is a subtle yet significant difference in the stance of those who draw a line in the sand and close down conversation by calling it conviction, and those who are willing to humbly draw that line in the sand until the high tide rolls in and wipes it out.

When we lay down the gauntlet and draw our line with statements like, "I will never . . ." we set ourselves up for a very difficult path ahead. The first obstacle is our natural pride. If I have told everyone I know that I will never do something, then it will take a lot longer to do it. Usually this is a good thing, but if I have told the world I would never do something and then realize I must, I have to eat some humble pie. And for me, this usually takes me longer than it should, and sometimes I even miss out on opportunities for my family because I am too proud to go back on my "never" statement.

Another self-imposed obstacle is the direction we have turned our eyes. We have this mythological destination to which we want to take our family, and with all the intention and conviction in the world we set out in that direction. The problem that few young parents realize, while all older ones know, is that children are not like other projects. They are humans with their own wills, desires, temperaments, and needs. There is no way to know when our child is 3, what sorts of issues will come up when they are 10, 15, or 20.

Instead of fixing our eyes down the road at our desired destination and marching with all our effort to this place, God sets up another framework in which to travel.

Along The Path We Are Given Only A Lamp

"Thy Word is a lamp unto my feet, and a light unto my path." Psalm 119:105

One of my favorite childhood songs is *Thy Word* by Amy Grant. It may sound cheesy, but whenever I think of this passage of scripture, I immediately go back to my childhood listening to "The Collection" and humming the tune (as I am right now). This is a great song, and does a great job at fleshing out one of the most powerful images in scripture as to what our journey with God looks like.

We often think of our journey with God in terms of a Google maps application. We feel God has given us some sort of picture or calling for our lives, then we punch in that destination followed by the "Directions From Here" button, and, like magic, we have a clear path to follow: God's Will!

While I do think that God gives us a calling and even a perceived destination, the application God chooses to use is a little more old school. Instead of a GPS unit, God offers us a lamp. It's been a long time since I walked with a lamp, but a recent camping trip reminded me of this unique mode of discerning a path.

A lamp doesn't illuminate the trail up ahead like a flashlight. A lamp simply reveals the next step or two. For the immediate future a lamp allows us to see where we are going, see and manage present obstacles, and read signs and markers that are right in front of us. All throughout scripture God keeps teaching this form of walking with Him, because it doesn't seem to make sense to us. God said He would provide manna to the Israelites every day, yet they hoarded it, and it went bad. Jesus brought this concept home in the Lord's Prayer when we ask for our daily bread. We only should ask for, work with, pray for, worry about, and wrestle with the concerns and issues that are a part of this day--the part of the path that God's lamp illuminates.

A lamp doesn't presuppose that we are aimless. There is a path and a direction. We simply stay daily connected to God, to our Lamp, and walk towards our desired destination. But because we are daily connected to Him, we will realize when we are starting to head in the wrong direction, and we'll be ready and willing to change course. We don't claim to know the entire road or the exact destination. We simply walk with conviction towards where we think God is leading us, one step at a time. And because all we get to see is the next two or maybe three, we must be humble and open to where the final destination will be.

What Does God Have For Us Today? Maybe Tomorrow?

In the same way this section began, it also ends. Being a parent of toddler doesn't mean we have to have all the answers, or tread water until our kids are old enough to go to school and give us a break. Rather it simply means that now, more than ever, we must practice the presence of God.

Practicing the presence of God is most important as we try to discern the direction and calling that God has placed on us individually and as a family. But asking God to reveal this to us once, fixing our eyes on those goal posts and move unwaveringly toward them is a recipe for disaster. We must continue to reorient our map, and change our view of the journey. We are not in a family car racing down the freeway toward our destination; rather we are holding hands, walking through the forest at night with a lamp for our feet.

In this second picture we must live differently, talk differently, and ask different questions. We humbly draw lines in the sand, we hold loosely on to plans and positions, and we allow our children to become their own people. We get back to the basics of asking for our daily bread and our daily steps, and then are thankful when God shows up and provides. We backtrack when we realize we have made a wrong turn and call for help from God and from our community to navigate our way back to the path.

We must be open to what God has, not just for our future and us, but also for our individual children with their unique and amazing talents, needs, abilities, and handicaps. Every season of life brings different challenges. What our family needs today will of course be different five years from now. Asking God, or worse telling God what our life will look like and what our kids' lives will look like in the future is just plain silly. Planning for the next year, five years, or twenty years probably just causes God to laugh. Rather than driving our car full speed toward an outdated destination for our family, it might be time to pull the car over and walk hand in hand through the woods relying on the daily illumination and provision of God.

It is for this reason that we must continue to ask, "God, what do you have for us today, and maybe tomorrow?"

Questions for Reflection:
1) What are some of the "nevers" you have for your children?
2) What do you think God's calling is for your family?
3) Are you driving full speed on your own strength and insight? How can you slow down?
4) What can you do to begin to walk towards that destination?
5) Who are people that can help you discern the path?

section three:
VITAL RHYTHMS FOR SPIRITUAL GROWTH

chapter one: YOU CAN'T PASS ON WHAT ISN'T YOURS

A Light bulb Just Went On

"My son is totally out of control! This is not the way we raised him."

This heartfelt cry came in the middle of a really difficult conversation with a parent from our church. What started out as a lighthearted lunch, discussing our recent adventures, turned into one of the deepest, most heartfelt, reflective conversations I have had with a parent in a long time.

Soon into our meal, this parent began to lament the choices their oldest son was making. He had gotten into a group of friends who seemed to be pulling him in all the wrong directions. He was recently caught lying about some significant things, and he was involved with a young woman in a way that had become difficult to turn a blind eye to. He didn't seem to care about his faith or his future.

The more my friend processed the heartbreak of watching his son distance himself from the family, lamenting the fact that he never really found a home at our church or student ministry, the more a light seemed to go on. What helped illuminate the conversation was the stark contrast in trajectory their oldest son was on compared to the one their two younger kids were taking.

Just as the conversation began to dive into despair and hopelessness, this parent did what few parents ever do in regards to their own children: he began to reflect on his own parenting; how he had parented his oldest so much differently than his younger children. You see, when he was a brand-new parent, his own faith was not very developed. The choices, values, and decisions he made as a first-time parent were barely impacted by his infant faith.

As their second and then third child came along, both this dad and his wife had undergone a spiritual renewal, becoming very serious about their faith. From almost day one of their younger children's lives, faith had been an integral part of their family rhythm.

What is amazing to me is that, with just a four-year head start, the rhythms were already in place for their oldest son to be on a road leading to questioning, and even rebellion, while their other two children saw the church as an extension of their family and a place where they belonged.

Soon after the light came on, I could tell that the dad was about to take a nosedive as he pulled out a final club to beat himself with. "If only we had figured this out earlier, and plugged our oldest into the church sooner, or made faith a more central part of our lives earlier on, our son wouldn't be in this situation."

After walking through hundreds of conversations like this one, I've come to realize that there is no magic pill or silver bullet that guarantees a child will embrace the faith of their parents. There are too many variables and mysteries that go into this. But one thing seems to be pretty consistent: kids will almost always accept the *values* of their parents.

It was with this truth I was able to encourage my friend. Although their oldest son missed out on some of the initial faith formation, their family values had been evident since he was born. The fact that the parents came to faith later in life and had spent the last decade seeking Jesus, wrestling with how their faith impacts their lives, spoke of their family values of teachability and integrity. These values were being passed on to their kids, and because their family oozes humility and kindness, they had made a huge onramp for their oldest son to continue to be part of their family. By living for Christ, the parents were making the case that faith in Jesus is a viable option for their son someday if he chooses it.

Your Kids Reflect You

As I mentioned before, I've walked through the chaos of adolescence with hundreds of families. And you would think that after doing this for as long as I have, I would have discovered some sort of trick to passing on faith. While the formula continues to elude me, I have found a rule that is rarely broken: no matter what, families will pass on the core of who they are.

I have seen many families attempt to sugarcoat this reality, or conceal it with great showmanship. But no matter how many good things we do, or how many words we use to express our desired values, in the end, our core values and beliefs are what get passed on to the next generation.

In the Christian world I have seen the attempt to pass on faith by using words to shape and spin events, when the actions taken scream that this spoken faith is not actually a core value or belief. It looks like:

A mom, very good at teaching her daughter songs and bible verses about the goodness of God and how we are to trust Him with our entire lives, pulls her out of school two months into kindergarten because of an overwhelming fear of the public school system.

A mom is a huge John Eldredge fan and wants more than anything for her little boy to grow into a godly man who able to handle all the adventure life throws his way. While she uses endless words to affirm this truth, every action screams that he is fragile and incapable of managing play dates, scrapes, and even food.

A dad being extra intentional about time with his son in order to make sure his boy knows how much he is loved and how he will never leave or forsake him. And this time has become more intense since he has recently separated from his wife, proving that there really is little security he can offer.

A mom who very intentionally sets aside time to pray and read the bible with her kids and makes sure they come to church every week is then heard ripping apart the pastor and others at the church, making the church an unsafe place that even parents don't trust.

Maybe one reason so many kids walk away from their faith is that what has been communicated did not match the actual values and actions lived out day in and day out within the family. Your life is the true representation of what you believe. If you are all about behavior management, rules-driven, if you are passive, mean, fearful, rude, prideful—then no matter what you say, this is what will get passed on.

We Can Not Pass On Our Desires

The unfortunate reality is that we cannot pass our desires to our kids. If we could, we would be set. I have huge desires for myself, my wife and for my family. I imagine coming home from work and being so excited to engage my family, play Legos with my son and tea with my daughter. My desire is that they know, without a doubt, that they are of utmost value to me and that they have my undivided attention. My desire is to help them develop a faith that is deep and transformative and to share special prayer time with them as I tuck them into bed. More than anything, I desire to pour out my entire life and all my love and affection into my precious kids.

But my desires don't rule the day. My real life and real actions do. Instead of coming home all ready to pour my life into my kids, I actually get home tired and in need of some space and quiet. The problem is that this is the exact opposite of what my kids need. For all my desires to get on the floor and open up the box of Legos, I sit on the couch and turn on the TV. Instead of thinking about all the special ways we can soak up these precious few hours of time together, all I am really doing is counting down until bedtime. And when bedtime does actually roll around, my desire for intimate sharing and prayer time gets thrown out the window, as tucking in my kids becomes an exercise in efficiency.

At the end of the day, what I have passed on to my kids are not my desires for them to know how valuable they are to me, but that they are in effect afterthoughts and leftovers. And the faith that is so important and transformative to me, the faith I so desire to pass on to them, may actually get communicated to them as empty traditions and words.

This reality scares me to death. I shudder to think that my kids will end up like so many of the students who have walked through my student ministry. These students have come from solid Christian families, from parents who had a genuine faith of their own, but somehow managed to pass on a powerless religion with boring rituals to their children.

If I will pass on the core of who I am, then I need to get "who I am" in order. I am not content with passing on a fake, sugarcoated version of myself or of my faith, a faith that has dramatically transformed and healed me. I am not content with passing on empty words and irrelevant traditions to my kids. Since kids have an amazing way to cut through all of the fluff and see the core of who we are, then I must continue to work out my faith, making sure it's alive and vibrant, and not simply give lip service of it to my children.

Developing a Faith That is Real and Vibrant

The problem is that it feels impossible to make space to develop a faith that is alive and vibrant when your little kids are running around screaming and not sleeping when they are supposed to. But as I mentioned before, in this season there is little to no space to maintain our faith through traditional quiet times. A solution is to practice the presence of God in the day-to-day realities of life, seeing the entire day as sacred rather then one tiny part that is practiced in private.

While this is a solution in expressing a vibrant faith, the other question is, "What are the rhythms that you can incorporate into your life that will actually develop your faith?" The truth is, there are various rhythms that Christians have used for thousands of years to keep them grounded, connected to God and used by God to mold, shape, and transform people. The ones we will look at in the next few chapters are corporate worship, fellowship, Sunday school, and family devotions.

But before we explore these rhythms further, we must first come face to face with the real faith and values we are attempting to pass on to our children. It is only then that we can move forward and use these other rhythms to develop a thriving faith and not just be a collection of hollow traditions.

Our bodies are a great example of how our desires don't always match up with our actions. For my entire adult life I have tried to lose 30 lbs. Have you ever geared up for a diet, committing to finally lose that holiday weight, baby weight, depression weight, or just plain lazy weight? No matter how it got there, you decide in your heart of hearts that you are done. After deciding to lose the weight, you commit to a few solid disciplines that will help you achieve your goal.

For as long as I can remember, my heart's desire has been to have a good body. The reality is that I don't. Because of this tension between my desire and the reality I find myself in, I am in a never-ending diet cycle. My diet works when I commit to a plan and then actually do it for a consistent amount of time. Sure enough, in just a matter of weeks my body begins to transform. But whenever I deviate from this plan, my body doesn't change at all, or returns to its former unhealthy state.

This reality is also true with our faith development as well. The results do not come overnight. A vibrant faith happens when we commit to the disciplines and rhythms that place our families and us where the Holy Spirit can grab hold of our hearts and transform us. It is the continual implementation of these rhythms that develops and grows a genuine faith, a faith that we want to actually share with our kids.

The question is, what actually gets passed on to our kids? Just like my body is the evidence of what I truly believe about my diet, our kids' lives and faith are a reflection of what we truly believe, value and are committed to. Faithful dedication to sacred rhythms is what develops a vibrant faith. And it is only when we have an active, growing, and reflective faith will we be able to pass on an actual faith and not religiosity to our children.

Today is as Good as any to Begin

There is no wrong time to start; no date is too late.

When are you going to start this new rhythm? New Years? The start of school? After vacation? Instead of continually kicking this down the road to the next milestone, why not just start right now? Pray with your family tonight. Go to church this Sunday. Spend time with a family who shares your passion for God this week.

The only way to screw this up is by not starting at all. Even if you have been delinquent in sharing a vibrant faith to your kids up until now, actually starting communicates important values to your kids as well. It is as important to share your journey with your kids, why you haven't developed a rhythm before, and why you are now, as it is to actually start. Share why you have tried and why you have failed and why you will continue to try and fail. Failing is a fact of life, so sharing the acts of trying and failing and trying again, moving a little further down the road each time, teaches dramatic lessons over never trying at all, or trying once, failing and quitting.

Our kids have an amazing way of cutting through all the fluff and surface paint of our lives, and recognizing our true family values and beliefs. We parents must do some hard work to reflect on what our lives and actions are actually communicating to our children. And if we are going to pass on a vibrant faith, a faith that is alive and actually transforms, then we must make sure we develop the rhythms in our lives that connect us to God and God's people.

TODAY IS THE DAY!

Questions for Reflection:
1) What values and beliefs did you get from your parents?
2) What desires did your parents express that you rejected?
3) If your kids reflected your true beliefs and values, what would they reveal?
4) What are your immediate excuses for not committing to church? Small groups? Sunday school, etc?

chapter two: REDISCOVERING THE PURPOSE OF CORPORATE WORSHIP

My First Apartment

Do you remember your first apartment? Where was it located? How was it decorated? Where did you scrounge up the furniture? How much did you pay in rent? Who did you live with?

When I chose my first apartment there were only two factors that went into the decision-making process. First was choosing who I would live with. Once that was decided, there was only one rubric to measure all our options against: how much was it going to cost?

The cost and the cost alone was the sole determining factor of where I would decide to sign on the dotted line. For $280 a month, I was able to forgo an apartment all together and upgrade to a 2000 square foot house that 12 of us fit into. I am sure that had to be breaking some sort of health code, but at the time, health codes were the least of my worries.

This group of friends and I begged, borrowed, and stole (OK, maybe not stole, but creatively borrowed) to furnish this place. I found a chair on the side of the road that I thought would work perfectly to watch TV. And it did, except once it was inside we noticed it was leaking and the cushions were home to several species of insects.

The sad thing is that as I graduated from college, got a job, and got married, I took this same perspective in apartment shopping into every new season. Now, instead of me being the only person making the decision and cost being the only true factor, I had to consider somebody else and take into account their factors. And what I soon realized is that my value of frugality—well, really *cheapness*—did not sit well with my wife's value of safety and security.

When it came time to raise a family and buy a house the factors begin to multiply. What would work fine for me, and barely work for my wife, wouldn't work at all for raising a family. A realtor friend of mine said that when young families are looking for a home they almost all have the same three important considerations: a good school district, a yard, and a safe street.

None of these factors even mattered to me when I chose my first, second, and third apartments. But once I was married and had little children of my own, I had to take all these factors into account to find a place where to land for the long haul.

For the most part, families are very intentional with choosing where they are going to land when it comes to their housing. However, I've noticed that very few families are as intentional about choosing where they will land when it comes to worship.

Choosing a Church For the Long Haul

There are a million reasons people choose churches, and depending on their current felt needs, those reasons can change. But usually most of those reasons center on some theme revolving around what a church does or doesn't do for me.

I do think it is of utmost important to find a church that meets you where you're at, connects you to Jesus, and moves you on path towards being transformed into His likeness. But I have often found that the church that "does it" perfectly for me often doesn't work perfectly for my wife. And the church that works great for us as a couple may not work if they lack attention and focus towards children and students.

As a pastor I've seen tons of families come and go for a wide variety of reasons. But most of the transitions that happen for families happen when parents begin to realize that church is not just for them but for their children also. Some of the greatest and hippest churches for young professionals come up short when it comes to providing care and formation for their kids. Most parents will tolerate a below-average children's church until they realize that this below-average attention happens for children all the way to students.

If you choose a church solely for you and not for the needs of your entire family, at some point the pull to leave will be too much. When families leave churches, even for the sake of their children, there are often deep repercussions within the hearts of the children. It can even feel painfully like a divorce, couched in really spiritual-sounding rhetoric.

Just as it is important to choose a housing option that is appropriate for where you are right now in life as a family--a place where kids can land, thrive, build community, and find safety--the same is true when finding a church. When your kids are little, that is the time to find the community of people who share your heart and values for worship, as well as the community that will provide excellent care for kids throughout their entire childhood.

Worship Is Different With Kids

Before kids I loved church and I was actually able to engage God during worship and focus during the sermon. But now, it takes all our energy just to get the family up and out the door even to make it on time to church. And even if we succeed in making it to church on time, I have found that the closer we are to being on time, the more conflict we experienced on our way.

Maintaining the value of corporate worship with little kids is one of the biggest challenges we have faced. Even as a pastor at the church it sometimes is easier for my wife to stay behind than fight all the battles to get there. I couldn't even imagine sacrificing one of my precious days off for the death and destruction of getting the entire family out the door before 10:00 am.

Getting to church is actually only the first hurdle in getting to a place where I can encounter God in corporate worship. Once we get to church then we have to check in with the nursery. We sign in, explain the particular issue or rash that is going on with each kid, take our beepers and head off into church.

Now, easily 20 minutes late, it's hard to find a seat and it feels like everyone is staring us as we self-consciously sit down. Throughout the entire service I find my heart divided. I feel guilty for not being able to engage in church, I feel worried about the care my child is receiving, and I am second-guessing whether or not it was even a good decision to show up in the first place. With this mindset, the chance of me actually getting anything out of worship is almost nil. Which leads me to the most important point.

Corporate Worship is Not About Me

Even though I know in my head that this is true, it wasn't until I had children that I actually had to come to terms with this reality. Before kids, we fool ourselves by thinking we are great and selfless people, but once we have children we realize there is a battle for the center, and we are losing! This transfer of power from us to our children is noticeable in where we choose to live, the cars we buy and the shows we now watch on TV.

This transition is right and normal. All along we should have already been wrestling with our egos, and killing our pride and our need to be the center of the universe. Corporate worship is one of the most important times when we must come to terms with us not being the center. It sounds so spiritual to talk about how church isn't deep enough for me, or the music isn't spiritual enough for me, or whatever the issue—it isn't good enough for me.

But the joke is on us, because none of it is really for me. Or, not really just for me. We need to find a place where we can land that will nurture not only my own faith, but the faith of my entire family. Once we do, then it is time to stay put and do some hard work.

I say "hard work" because corporate worship is the number one vital rhythm for spiritual growth. It is the place where Christians gather to learn, build community, and worship the living God.

Corporate worship reminds that we are no longer the center of the universe: *God is.*

Corporate worship reminds us who is in charge of the world: *Not me!*

Corporate worship reminds us who provides our daily needs: *Jesus does.*

Corporate worship reminds us that we do not participate in a dead religion: *We are invited to be connected to and transformed by the living God!*

I know that in the midst of all the chaos that surrounds getting to, sitting through, and coming home from church, these truths are easy to miss. But if we miss them, then we prove that we are really participating in empty religious tradition, not nurturing and developing a faith that is central to our lives.

It is a myth that we don't need corporate worship to grow in our faith. Now, if our faith is in ourselves then yes, we don't need church. But if our faith is in Jesus Christ, then we must do the tougher work and show up. People always ask why they need to go to a building to worship God? And, why can't we worship God at our homes? Yet I have never met the family that actually intentionally worshiped God at home without the support and direction that happens from church.

And while I call including corporate worship in our weekly rhythm "hard work," we can implement some patterns and routines that allow us to get to church without too much drama.

5 Easy Ways To Actually Encounter God in Corporate Worship

1) Make getting to church a win. Nobody wants to wake up early on the weekend and go to church, especially your kids. Cartoons and pajamas will always win. But if you can develop a special routine for Sunday mornings, then the day and the event get set apart in your kids' eyes as special, even sacred. We found that food is the best way to make this happen. And because both my wife and I have to now be at church every week, we found that making a trip to the donut shop is a great way to celebrate the fact that it is a church day. I know it is dangerously close to a bribe, but after a couple of years, donuts make Sunday mornings a win.

2) Show up early. I know we already went over how difficult it is to even get to church. But once you decide that church is a value, you will actually find a way to get there. You make it to work on time, to preschool on time, to the airport on time. It's simply a matter of making it a priority. If you can do that with church, then the rushed chaos of the morning gets replaced with a calm check-in, visiting with friends, and settling in for the entire service. There is a lot of work that goes into the planning the entire service. When you are there from the beginning you have a way better chance to actually encounter God as the worship leaders move you through the service.

So find some ways to make Sunday morning go smoothly. Choose and lay out clothes Saturday night with the help of your kids. Find a way to make breakfast quick and easy (there's that donut shop idea again!). Be realistic about how long it takes you to get all of you ready and out the door, then add 15 minutes to your time to anticipate one last diaper change or spilled coffee. Breathe.

3) Ask God to show up. This seems like a no-brainer, but even as a pastor I often forget this one. The truth is that God is already there and of course He will show up. But even though God is at work all around us, it is easy to miss it. Asking God to show up is my simple prayer that reminds me to keep my eyes and heart open to the things of God and the ways that He might want to move in and through me. It is like being completely silent. The longer we are quiet the more we can hear. The more we are expectant in our prayers for God to show up, the more we can actually see when He does. And doing this as a family—at the breakfast table, or in the car in the driveway before we back out--models this anticipation and awareness to our kids.

4) Take notes. I am not talking about writing down a shopping list or a list of to do's as your mind wanders during the sermon. I am talking about the discipline of active listening. Just as when you were in school, when taking notes solidified in your mind what you were hearing, so it will in church. Your pastor has put 10-15 hours of work into the sermon you are listening to. He didn't want to just get up there and ramble. God actually put specific things on his heart as he studied that particular passage of scripture and I bet some of it might actually be just for you. Taking notes then allows you to focus in on what is being said and what you might actually be convicted about and need to put into practice.

5) Actually try to implement one thing. The biggest crime is for a roomful of people to walk into church, sing songs, listen to a sermon, and walk out the door acting like nothing ever happened. The Christian life is about connecting with the living God and being transformed into His likeness. This process of transformation takes work. It usually begins with the Holy Spirit convicting us about something, then being faithful to do that something. After I have been convicted, I usually quickly forget all about it. But if I write it down, remember it, then actually do it, I am partnering with the Holy Spirit in His process of transformation and sanctification.

Corporate worship is not, and never has been, about us. Once we find a place that will work for the spiritual nurture and growth for our entire family, it is time to lock it down and determine in our hearts that worshipping here is a value for our family. Once that decision is made, then the rest of it is easy. By maintaining the discipline of corporate worship we can actually reorient our worldview, place God back in His rightful place as center, and be open to the invitation of worship, friendship, healing and transformation that happens every Sunday at 10:00 AM.

Questions for Reflection:
1) When you were only responsible for yourself, where did you choose to live? Choose to worship?
2) Does your house now or your church reflect the values and needs of your entire family?

3) What is a stumbling block that is keeping you from committing to a rhythm of corporate worship?
4) Try the 5 easy ways to encounter God and write down how God actually showed up.

chapter three: PUTTING THE SCHOOL BACK IN SUNDAY SCHOOL

It is Hard Teaching My Kids to Read

Have you ever seen those ads on TV that boast how they can teach your infants and toddlers to read? They are compelling advertisements, with kids younger than mine reading books. If only my son could read at a 5th grade level before he begins kindergarten he would be on track to have a successful academic career. So, after catching just the end of the commercial, I was hooked. It only took coming across the commercial one more time during Saturday morning cartoons before my credit card was out and I was locked in to 20 easy payments of $19.99.

When the box arrived, I was a little overwhelmed by the size. I thought there would be a small package with a few DVDs. But it turns out putting your kid in front of a TV and the DVDs would turn them into a genius was just the 30 second version. For your child to get the full impact of the product you had to do flash cards, sight words, memorization, and writing for 30 minutes a day. Immediately I knew I was in over my head. Within a week I knew this wasn't going to work. So I packed it all back in its original box and "returned to sender."

This commercial messed me up more than I realized. I now was fixated on my son's intellectual development, and worried that he would fall behind. As I dropped him off at preschool one day, I overheard some parents talking about "Bob" books. I had never heard of them, but before I had even gotten to my car I bought the entire series off of Amazon.

Now Bob books were something I could get behind. They are these tiny books that teach only a few words at a time and are written in a way that makes it easy to find success. Success until I realized that my son was two series behind. So when I accelerated his reading, our special time together became a disaster. I finally gave up and determined it was better to have a good relationship with my son who might never learn to read than have him go to Harvard at 9 years old.

This past year my son completed his first year in Kindergarten. And I must confess, I was blown away with what happens at school. At school they had a time-tested plan and a proven curriculum to teach my son how to read. And not only how to read, but count to 100, do math, and explore science. Who knew? And the best part was that his teacher gave him homework so that he could continue to work on these blossoming skills at home. Now our evenings became a win, as we worked together to memorize sight words and fill in counting pages. And sure enough, by the end of his Kindergarten year, he reads at a first grade level. Amazing!

The Church Is Supposed to Do It

For almost the entire history of Christendom, it was the church that was tasked with passing on the faith from one generation to the next. For both the Catholic tradition as well as many mainline Protestant churches such as Presbyterians and Lutherans there have long been very intentional rhythms for faith development. It began when a family in the church brought their baby to be baptized. In this sacrament of baptism both the family and the church were affirming God's gracious hand on this child and celebrating the fact that this child's identity was a part of this particular Christian community.

A baby's baptism was not supposed to affirm that this child now was a Christian, or guaranteed to go to heaven. Rather, it was an agreement that the church would teach and pass on the Christian faith, and the parents would model this faith and help them put it into practice. Depending on the tradition of the church, as early as first grade, the child would begin catechism classes. In fact this year in my son's first grade class a dozen kids are beginning CCD, the catechism classes in the Catholic Church. In other traditions the catechism class might be called confirmation and be done in middle school.

No matter what it was called or when it was done, the premise was that since birth God had had His hand on this baby, but at some point the child would need to make their faith their own, or "confirm" the faith that was affirmed by their parents. Historically in both the Catholic and mainline traditions, it was the church who was responsible for the teaching. But during the early 1900's this rhythm began to change.

For a wide variety of reasons the Evangelical church with its emphasis on personal salvation and believer's baptism became the dominant voice in our American Christian culture. And during this transition there was a not-so-subtle shift that occurred in our understanding of faith development and discipleship. The church suffered the same fate as just about every institution in the US: a growing lack of confidence in the effectiveness of the institution coupled with a growing emphasis on the individual rather than the group or community.

While this shift has affected our entire cultural view regarding the benefit of institutions or institutional membership, it has dramatically impacted our view of the church and the job of faith formation within our children. No longer is the church viewed as the responsible entity to teach children about their faith; that is now the job of the family. The family unit is now the place where faith begins and is nurtured. The church then becomes a place that at best accentuates what is being taught at home, and at worst a serves as a glorified babysitter while the important formation happens for parents in "big church."

How we got to this place is complex, and not really the point. My observation is, after several generations of this model of faith development, we have arrived in a place that is the worst of both models. There is a lack of value in the church and the "official" teaching of the church with little commitment to Sunday school, confirmation, or catechism. And to make it worse, there is a lack of ability of parents to pull it off. And because the parents lack the ability, they are insecure and passive in their role because they are uncertain with what to teach, how to do it, and whether it is even effective.

Many parents I know feel the same, if not worse, about the faith development of their children as I did attempting to teach my son how to read, with zero understanding of the process or tools available. Maybe it is time to re-engage the church and find a happy medium between the ancient church-taught faith that is historical, complex, and deep, and the family that nurtures this faith and proves it to be relevant and vibrant.

Put the School Back in Sunday

Even though I am a pastor and a huge part of my job is overseeing our children's ministry at our church, I am first and foremost a dad who feels just as insecure and lost in terms of the best ways to help my kids nurture and develop a faith that is their own. In a similar vein with the learning-to-read fiasco, I have done just as many silly things with my kids while attempting to help them figure out their faith as well.

I have bought just about every child's Bible on the market; I have kids' worship music, biblical craft packs, Bible Man DVDs and whatever else is in the children's section at the Christian Book store. And while all of these investments have been beneficial and have helped our kids learn some Bible stories and characters, I still can't shake the knot I have in my stomach from all the anxiety of not doing it right.

We don't have to live with this never-ending anxiety. There is actually some good news right in front of you. It is the children's ministry at your local church. You don't need to buy extra books, go to special seminars or buy more children's bibles. All you have to do is put the school back in your Sunday.

I am pretty sure that the church you attend has a children's ministry plan. There is an actual person whose entire job, whether paid or volunteer, is to think about the faith development of your child and to put together a curriculum that is age-appropriate for them. They have a one-year, three-year, or even a six-year plan that teaches the basics of the Christian faith in an organized manner. And the best part is that it is done in a way that is fun.

Besides what is actually taught on a Sunday morning, there are usually take-home sheets or crafts that accompany your child when you pick them up. These sheets were not done so your children's workers would have job security. These are practical, age-appropriate take-homes that give you as a parent a place to begin as you continue to help your child develop their own faith.

It is sad that it took me a few years to realize how helpful all these tools are for me in passing on my faith to our kids. I wrongfully thought that, because I was a pastor and my entire job is helping kids and students develop their faith, I would not need any outside support for my own kids. Thankfully, I have become a true believer in Sunday school, not just as a pastor, but also as a parent.

Just as "real" school has staff, curriculum, a plan, and resources to actually teach my children all the academics they need to know, Sunday school does exactly the same for my kids' faith. And just like in real school, if I don't engage the subjects that are taught in class and reaffirm the lessons in his homework time, then those concepts don't sink in, and sure enough he will fall behind. School works best when both parents and the school partner in the academic development of your child. When the parents and church partner up for the faith development of your child, the chances for success explode.

An Amazing Curriculum

I don't know what curriculum your church uses, but our church recently has begun to use a curriculum called **Orange** (www.whatisorange.org). The basic idea of Orange is that parents and the church should synchronize their efforts to pass on a real and vibrant faith to the next generation. Orange happens when the Yellow light of the church combines with the Red love and nurture of the family. Orange is both a curriculum and a strategy. And because of this, I have found it to be an amazing resource no matter how much your particular church chooses to use their specific curriculum.

While I fully endorse Orange's curriculum and am blown away by the way they communicate faith to my kids in such a fun and relevant way, there are many curriculums that accomplish this goal. And just like Orange, any curriculum of value will have parents' packs and resources so parents can follow up to combine efforts in the faith development of your children.

Being a father of two little kids, I need the benefit of someone else doing the hard work of developing a curriculum plan, follow-up questions, and places to put that into practice. Through this curriculum, and hopefully the one used by your church, I have all the tools at my disposal to take the best resources and teaching of the church and combine it with the unique love, passion, and faith of our family so together we have the best chance possible for faith to be passed on to the next generation.

It is easy to affirm the local school and its central importance to the academic development of our children.

Because this value is so important, we have all chosen to structure our entire lives around it. We plan our days, structure our vacations, and even choose a bedtime based on the 8:00-3:00, M-F, 180 days of school in the academic year. The more we move in sync with this value, the better off our kids will be academically.

When we consider the faith development of our children, would there be a similar value and emphasis? Having our kids develop a faith that is alive and vibrant has to become not just a verbalized value, but one that is proven valuable by our rhythms of life. We do not have to, and are not supposed to be, the sole provider of faith to our children. We know this to be true academically, now we just need to embrace this truth spiritually. And may God be gracious to us as we struggle and succeed at partnering more and more with our church communities so that our kids, too, may become women and men who love and trust God with their whole hearts, to be used by Him in amazing ways.

Questions for Reflection:
1) What rhythms do you have at home that help affirm the value of faith?
2) Do you know what curriculum your church uses? Do you help or volunteer within your children's ministry? Why or why not?
4) Where do you land on the spectrum between the church or the family being responsible for passing on the Christian faith?
3) What would happen if you treated Sunday School like normal school?
4) Commit to pick up, read, and implement the take-home sheet given out by your children's ministry.

chapter four: BIBLE STUDIES AND BILLIARDS

Some Things Never Change

When I was in college I worked with middle-schoolers as their Lead Counselor at a Christian Summer Camp. This by far was, and still is, one of the sweetest times of my life. Being a part of a team of people who worked together 24/7 to help middle-schoolers have an amazing time and create space for them to encounter the Lord was both exhausting and rewarding. As the summer progressed, I began to realize that much of the reward was living vicariously through some of my teammates, specifically the female Lead Counselors.

You see, every night after campfire we would gather together in sections. These sections were divided into one, two, or three boy sections, and one, two, or three girl sections. This was an opportunity to check in one last time, pray together, and then give directions to our counselors as they took their kids back to the cabin for cabin talks.

Once we were finished with our circle prayer, the lead counselors would meet up in the dining hall for our evening meeting. At this meeting we would raid the kitchen, make grilled cheese sandwiches, laugh about the silly things our kids did, go over plans for the next day, and pray for our kids and counselors by name, then go to bed just to do it all over again in a few short hours.

It didn't take much time for a discernible pattern to begin to emerge. As the week progressed, the female lead counselors would show up later and later, while us male lead counselors would eat more and more grilled cheese. Half way through the summer we had enough! What in the world was going on in their prayer circles that were adding another hour to the bedtime routine? We finally got the courage to ask our colleagues and we were shocked by what we heard.

They began to share story after story of middle school girls breaking down crying, others supporting them as they shared about family difficulties, wayward lifestyles, and how they desperately wanted Jesus to come into their hearts and change them. By Thursday night at camp, week in and week out, the girls were having revival. As our friends shared with swollen eyes about their overwhelming encounters in ministry, one of them had the guts to ask us what we were doing while they were giving Billy Graham a run for his money.

It took a moment for us to find the best way to burst their bubble, but once one of us began to talk, the floodgates opened up and we had the opportunity to share a summer's worth of frustration. While the girls were sharing their deepest and darkest and were ready to head off to the mission field, our boys were having quite a different experience.

As our boys would circle up and the leaders would close their eyes tightly to pray, it would begin. It seemed to always start with a fart, then some giggling, then more farting and more giggling, and before you knew it everyone was screaming and laughing about the smell and mocking the offender. This would be considered a good night. On more difficult nights the laughing and farting would somehow immediately transition into Wrestle-mania! Which of course was really fun until some kid got a bloody nose, lost a tooth, or even broke an arm. If we were ever late to our counselor meeting it wasn't because of earnest prayer time, but because we were breaking up fights or cleaning up graffiti.

And with all the death and destruction lived out by middle-school boys at summer camp, the bottom line is that God did and continues to use places like camp to grab hold of kids' hearts. For young girls it often looked like crying your guts out with an entire cabin gathered around them for support. For boys it looked more like who could drink the most Tabasco sauce in one sitting. While it doesn't seem like they have much in common, the fact that middle-schoolers were together working out their faith in a way that made sense to them and their developmental journey, a way key to their spiritual growth. And even though these middle schoolers have now grown up and are respectable adults, the manner in which they gather is often similar to that time in middle school.

We Must Continue to Meet Together

Hebrews 10:25 says, "Let us not give up meeting together, as some are in the habit of doing, but let us encourage one another--and all the more as you see the Day approaching."

If we are going to make it to the very end, and still be running strong in our faith, then we must continue to meet together. All throughout scripture we find included the assumptions that we belong to each other (Romans 12:5), we are to bear with one another as to fulfill the law of Christ (Galatians 6:2), and that the way we love each other proves that we are followers of Jesus (John 13:35). Knowing that we are supposed to be in community is nothing new in Christian circles, but actually living it out is entirely a different story.

Part of the problem is that there is some misunderstanding of how we are to live in community. Many people immediately go to Acts 2 and read how we are to eat, pray, study scripture, have fellowship and share all we have in common. While this sounds great, there is little direction as to what we study or how we study it. How we pray and for how long? And what actually counts as fellowship? In the absence of direct scriptural revelation, it turns out there is a wide variety of acceptable avenues for meeting together.

For the beginning part of my marriage I actually thought there was only one way for there to be true fellowship, and that was in the form of a couples' small group. On the surface it seemed like this was the ultimate fulfillment of Acts chapter 2. We shared a meal, and then someone would share a devotional from scripture. After discussing the passage in a group we would share our prayer requests and if there were ways we could come through for each other, we would. Could it be any better?

The truth is I hated every second of it. Being in a small group made me feel trapped. Because of my job, the thought of being out another night of the week sapped all my energy, and to top it off, sitting in a circle, week after week, as people shared and often cried, was more than I could take. Was I in a middle school girls' cabin? I often fantasized about farting in the middle of our prayer time just to see what sort of reaction I would get. Now, don't get me wrong, small group bible studies are an amazing way for us to stay connected and for fellowship to happen. And many people (for the most part those more mature than me), find a ton of fulfillment in them.

Still Pretty Different in Our Fellowship Needs

After several years of pushing through in our small group, I finally had the guts to pull the ejection lever. As my wife and I talked about this decision, and the repercussions that might happen when a pastor on staff bails on his small group, we realized that we both had the same needs for prayer, study, and fellowship, but how we expressed those needs were completely different.

I actually think it is unfair the way God made men and women so dramatically different. As middle schoolers, girls were already to spend hours sharing, crying, praying, and supporting one another and we grown men still can't get there. But instead of being bitter at God or trying to express my life and faith in a way that is completely unnatural, both my wife and I are trying to live out this Acts chapter 2 version of connection in ways that work with the unique design with which God has made us.

Because girls have been connecting on deep and intimate ways since middle school, there are often plenty of opportunities for them. Besides the classic mixed small group, I have been really impressed with the variety of women's ministry options available. My wife has participated in DVD studies, Bible Study Fellowship, and several summer Bible studies with women. She always leaves these times encouraged in her faith. And what I find most interesting is that the very act of sharing deeply and caring for one another gives her a fresh awaking to the movement of God.

A ministry our church operates in partnership with several other churches is MOPS (Mothers of Pre-Schoolers). The highlight of my year is when I get to speak at our local group, and for a morning share in the delight and angst of being a parent of a preschooler. The depth of sharing and the way that these moms rally behind each other is truly an inspiration. It is the one small group that I wish I could participate regularly in. I think there is something totally raw about being a mom whose life has been totally rocked by the invasion of a baby. This enormous change seems to bring with it an added sense of authenticity and camaraderie. Whether it is the sleep depravation or the amazing food, something truly special happens during these meetings that would make the author of Acts proud.

While a small part of me does long for these deep times of sharing around a circle, the truth is, week in and week out I need a completely different version of Acts 2. In the several churches I have been involved in, I always start with some sort of traditional small group, but in every context I have managed to find a group of disenfranchised men who cannot connect in these small groups. While some of the reason may be that our wives always have more to say, circle-sharing simply isn't how we were made.

Once this small group of men finds each other, we then work together to hatch a plan to establish a fresh model for community living. And there is something about the local billiards hall that seems to capture our hearts. After we have made our best case for why we men cannot continue in this small group, and why it would be better if we just met together, the hard work of explaining the billiard hall begins. The truth is that even adult men, men who are fathers and are turning gray, are still middle schoolers at heart. I am not saying that we are not deep or not spiritual, I am simply arguing that the way in which we relate to each other and to God has looked, and continues to look differently.

If one of our wives ever showed up at the billiards hall and spied on our Acts 2 group, she would probably be shocked at our apparent lack of spirituality. How is four men playing pool and enjoying an ale spiritual? And I bet for that moment it wasn't spiritual at all, in the classical sense. But for the past 3 years, this same group of 4 men have been meeting together regularly. Together we have walked through job changes, marital conflict, a loss of a parent, and wrestling with God's plan for us and our family's lives. For me, this depth comes from doing life together week in and week out. We don't sit around the pool table and ask how we are doing with the Lord and take turns talking while the others nod. We laugh at each other; we argue over scripture and politics, and in the midst of that we share life--real life. This works because we are four men who love Jesus and love our families: it just so happens that we don't relate well in small circles.

It Doesn't Matter How, It Just Matters That It Happens

I know I painted a stereotypical picture of men and women, but that's because my wife and I, in this respect, are stereotypical. But I do realize that we are all made differently and have different ways in which we connect.

There is a group of women who meet monthly late on a Friday night and they call their group Naked Poker. My wife was invited to be a part of this group and the name sparked my interest. They chose Poker to sound tough, and Naked to be shocking. These are my kind of women. When they gather they spend the evening cooking together, and taking turns sharing about their lives and their faith, and every month it is deep and transformative. There is little structure except for a handful of friends who love each other deeply.

There are also a couple of guys I know who were made for the circle-sharing and prayer time, but prefer to do this with just men. Every Monday they meet for lunch at a taco shop and in a very deliberate manner they go through their liturgy or prayer, sharing about their job, their faith, and the new things God is up to in their life. Every week it is deep, spiritual, and intentional.

I know of a small group of families who have chosen to live in a covenant sort of relationship with each other. Their times together revolve around a family meal. By the end of their time together the kids are watching a movie and these parents share together their joys and concerns, and pray for one another as they daily walk through the mayhem of life.

There are many more examples of how people get together to encourage each other to run the race of faith so we will be faithful until the end. It is a danger when we put each other and ourselves in boxes of how faith is "supposed" to be expressed. I'm pretty sure that there is no right or wrong way for this Acts 2 life to be lived out, other than it must involve other people on this journey as well. If what you are doing is not working, find something that is. Maybe you need the freedom to try something a little more unconventional, or give your spouse the freedom to try something a little more unconventional. Whatever it may be, if it works for you, that's what matters.

We are all made uniquely, so it makes sense that we connect uniquely. If it is deeply in a circle, then circle up. If it is deeply during a game of 8 Ball, then rack 'em up. Just do not neglect meeting together as some are in the habit of doing, but instead let us encourage one another, and all the more as you see the day approaching!

Questions for Reflection:
1) What were the groups in your past where you have thrived spiritually?
2) What were the groups in your past where you have thrived personally?
3) Do those groups have anything in common? Could they?
4) If you could design the perfect group to live out Acts 2 with, what would it look like?

chapter five: ATTEMPTING THE FAMILY DEVOTIONAL

What's The Difference?

Have you ever had one of your child's friends over for a play date and almost immediately it goes south? They cannot agree on what to play or figure out how to share. The way in which we intervene says a lot about our values and beliefs. In our house we make our children defer to their friends because they are guests in our home, and we are trying to teach our kids the value of hospitality.

While the subtleties of being hospitable get lost on them, the way they've come up with to make it stick in their own minds is that whoever is the guest is the boss. This isn't exactly what we were trying to communicate, but it works. At least, it worked until our child went to another family's home for a play date and there was a difference of values from ours. For the other family, everything has to be *fair* and the parent spent most of their time refereeing the activity to keep it that way.

Keeping things fair was in direct conflict with our kids' value of hospitality, especially since they were excited to go to someone else's house and get a chance to be the boss! I know that this is a silly example, but from this point on, the issues and conflicts are only going to grow exponentially.

What do we do when our kids are exposed to mild conflicts like bad manners and horrible language, or dangerous ones like drug and alcohol use and abuse? We can't isolate our kids from a world that doesn't share our same values and worldview. We actually need the refining that happens when our kids are exposed to people different than themselves. It is good, natural, and right for us to have our children question why we do what we do. When these questions come up, it is another opportunity to re-affirm the faith and values of our family.

On the surface it often seems like most families in your community share similar values. Your houses are pretty much the same, as are the kinds of cars you drive, and the toys your kids have are similar. This similarity raises some difficult questions for your kids and might even raise them for you. If as Christians we are to be *in* the world and not *of* the world, then why do we look so much *like* the world?

Wrestling with this question is a life-long challenge, and one we should continually keep to the forefront. While this issue is deep and complicated, we cannot be overwhelmed by how well we are doing or how much we are failing to be set apart from the world around us. The biggest mistake we can do is take this call to be set apart and actually remove our kids from encountering anyone who is different from us. We actually need to wrestle through all of the implications of this question in front of our kids, and continue to be humble and teachable as we do.

When we do this, we will actually be prepared to communicate the bigger story and values of our family in a positive light, rather than comparing it against the negative values of their friends. What we communicate is a set of values that have their foundation in our faith in God and in the high calling we have been invited into as His children.

Incorporating our Family Story into God's Story

When we parent with behavior-management as the goal, we give our kids a limited vision of who they are and why what they do makes a difference. No matter what words we use, what we communicate is that our kids are to behave so they don't embarrass us. But, instead of making our status at church and among our friends the driving force why our kids behave well, we as parents have an opportunity to affirm the reality of God and the blessing and responsibility it is to be a part of His family.

By incorporating family devotions into the regular rhythm of your family you communicate with not just your words, but with your actions, the foundation for your kids' identities and how they are to live. We think that our kids will naturally figure out that we love God and because we do, they will too. But the truth is that faith is a difficult and mysterious thing.

Because God is invisible it makes sense that our kids will rarely, if ever, be able to put two and two together regarding their faith and their actions. And to only use times where they are in trouble or bed time to talk about things of faith, allows kids to miss out on one of the most valuable things we can pass down as parents: the fact that we too have a faith that is alive and dynamic, that we too are continually growing and working things out in that faith, and that we too celebrate the very tangible ways that God has shown up, answered prayers, and taken care of us and our families.

Family devotions can be a really sweet time in our day or week where we as a family get to model a dynamic faith. Hopefully part of our faith development involves spending time in scripture and in prayer, combined with seeking to put into practice what we learn from scripture. As we do this, other things will come up, like a need for confession or a desire for praise and adoration. A family devotion is simply sharing this experience with your entire family.

An intentional devotion allows a natural rhythm for our entire family to read scripture, pray, and put it into practice. We get to once again frame who we are as a family and how our family fits into the larger family of God. Our values, behaviors, and beliefs are not simply because mommy and daddy think they are important, but are actually from God who invites all of us to be His precious children. As children of God, princes and princesses of the King, we have unique blessings and responsibilities. Devotions are a time when this story gets told over and over again.

The worst lesson our kids can learn from us in our parenting, praying, and even our devotional life, is that we have it all together and are fully formed, and from a place of perfection we help them become all that God has for them. At some point they will figure out we don't have it all together, and if we present ourselves as such, we add significant dissonance to their understanding of us and of faith. But when we are quick to ask for forgiveness, share how we are learning and growing, share our own prayer requests and celebrate when God answers them, we model a life-long faith. By sharing our own weaknesses and areas of growth we also allow a mental place for our kids to put their own disappointments with us as they grow and need to sort out a faith that is separate from ours.

Top 5 Ways to Make Family Devotions a Disaster:

1) Have unrealistic expectations for your time. You have little kids. They have very limited attention spans and a very poor grasp on abstract concepts. Chances are that there will be many tangents, and you will find yourself in the wilderness. Instead of seeing these distractions and challenges as failure, live into and celebrate where your kids are. What is being said with your words is less important than what is being said with your actions and consistency.

2) Equate spiritual with somber. For whatever reason, we have equated being spiritual with being somber. Haven't you noticed that kids are never somber unless something is wrong? Kids love to laugh and have fun, and because of this, time with God as a family should reflect that. Family devotions are an opportunity to help shape the understanding that loving God is about living into the abundant, joyful life offered to us in Jesus.

3) Place too much emphasis on one devotion time. As you share prayer requests or what scripture means, it is natural and normal that your kids will say shocking things and have poor theology. It is not vital to correct every misstatement out of a fear that they will always have these views.

4) Place too little emphasis on one devotion time. The inverse is also a potential disaster. If we are too flip and don't help our kids take it somewhat seriously, then we will find ourselves creating a rhythm where they do not take prayer or God seriously. It is a difficult balance, but one that has to be worked out. It is like not helping our kids use silverware appropriately: they then are the kids in elementary school who still eat like cavemen.

5) Give up. The biggest disaster would be trying, failing, and never trying again. As much as it seems like it should be normal and natural for parents who love God to have intentional conversation with their kids so that they would love God, it sometimes feels next to impossible. The more you keep at it, the easier it becomes, and soon it will actually become a highlight of the day or week.

Top 5 Ways to make it a Success:

1) Make it light-hearted and fun. If your devotion time is too deep or you are expecting them to wrestle with difficult issues, then you have never done a devotional with a toddler. Little kids love to have fun, so the challenge is to actually make this time fun. The more active it is, the more fun it will be, and the shorter it is, the less chance there is for an adult to get frustrated and make it not fun in a hurry.

2) Keep it to one point. There is a lot of information packed into just a few verses of scripture. If we try to unpack too much we will lose what little attention we have. Most resources out there keep the family devotion to one simple point. If you don't use outside help, pick one scripture that has one point, or a story that has one clear point. I can barely remember one point after hearing a sermon. Let's give our kids a break and help them land on one simple point with one simple application.

3) Giving everyone an equal chance to share. Family devotions are not the time where we parents help our kids "get it." Family devotions are the time where we are people who are working out our own faith, but doing it together as a family. This means that we parents don't just ask questions and expect retention and transformation from our kids, but we share how we're retaining the one simple point and putting it into practice.

4) Pick the right time and place for you and your family. Every family is different and has different needs and different places that are special and sacred. Some families have family devotions every Sunday night. Once a week is all that is realistic to pull off and can manage, and that is sacred time. Other families prolong bedtime and everyone piles into a bed and does a devotional together there. And some families choose to do a devotional around a mealtime. Instead of fighting about manners or staring at each other, a family devotional gets to be an intentional use of that time. No matter when or where you do it, the trick is just making sure you *do* it.

5) Keep trying. It is impossible to remember every meal you ever had. In fact it is probably pretty difficult to remember even a dozen meals. But there is a good chance that you have had several meals every day for your entire life. The individual meals are not what's important to give you the energy for the day, it is the consistent daily intake of food that allows us to live and thrive. Very few family devotion times for us are deep and meaningful, but we are confident that the accumulation of them will help our kids develop their own vibrant, alive faith.

Questions for Reflection:
1) When you pray with your kids, do you ever share the places that you are growing in your faith with them?
2) Where is the time and place that would work for a consistent devotional time? How often is realistic?
3) Where are you going to go for resources to make this time a win?

conclusion: CONFESSIONS OF AN AVERAGE DAD

Writing this book has been the most humbling and challenging experiences of my life.

Vocationally I am the Pastor of Children and Students at a local church. This means that my entire job, day in and week out, revolves around the spiritual development of children. I spend all my office time developing strategies and plans to make faith relevant and significant for children and students. While their spiritual needs are actually very similar, the ways in which they experience faith and the rate at which they choose to work it out vary by age and by kid. It is a very challenging job at the same time it's completely rewarding and fulfilling.

Outside of my office I spend the majority of my time meeting with parents who are at their wits' ends with their children. While part of the problem often has to do with a breakdown in parenting, I have realized that there is a deeper current running below the surface in almost every parent I talk to. Somewhere along the way their once passionate and vibrant faith has become dry and brittle.

Over and over I have talked with parents who are exhausted, out of ideas and in desperate need of wisdom. A quick fix seems to be a talk with a pastor, or to send their kid to counseling. But the more I meet with parents, the more I realize that it has been a long time since these parents were in the driver's seat when it comes to their lives and especially when it comes to their faith.

It used to be so easy as a childless pastor to meet with these parents, hear their stories, and try my best to help them navigate the bigger issues and provide pat answers about the need for the parents to care for their own walks with God as well. But now that I have my own kids, my world has been rocked! I am right in the middle of holding on to my life and my faith with hands that are cramping up. In fact, holding on has gotten tougher and tougher and the thought of letting go has gotten easier and easier.

Part of the reason for writing this book is because I needed to figure out some way to regain my own passionate pursuit of Christ in the midst of my precious kids who were sucking me dry. For several years I relied on experiences and the depth of knowledge and faith from my past. But quickly my tanks were becoming empty and the tree of faith was withering with little or no fruit to show. Remember the fruit of the Spirit? Love, joy, peace, patience, kindness, goodness, faithfulness, gentleness, and self-control? At an alarming rate these were disappearing from my life. My kids began to question why I was always unhappy or always had my "mean face" on. As I wrestled with the reason, I quickly realized that my faith had atrophied.

My belief in God and my love for Jesus never waned, but the connection had been broken. I was relying on my memory of faith rather than actually continually working it out, even in this chaotic season. And I realized that if I, a pastor, was experiencing this, then it was undoubtedly true for many of, if not most of, the parents I encountered every day.

Then one day it hit me--people in all places and in all times have found some way to work out their faith in Jesus. A designated quiet time for an hour at Starbucks is actually not the norm. Living every moment of every day connected to God, being sensitive to the places where God shows up, and responding to that truth, is. It doesn't matter if you lived in ancient Palestine and spent your entire day on a boat fishing or farming, or if you live now and your entire day is consumed with the raising of a toddler. Life has been, and will always be, hectic and out of control.

What we **can** control is the manner in which we engage our lives, and the intention we bring to our circumstances. My old rhythms are long gone, and the things that used to bring me such refreshment and renewal in my faith are distant memories. But I will not let my faith wither and die because this season is behind me. I must do what adults have done before me and live into this next season of life and faith.

To nurture and grow a tree of faith that bears the fruit of the Spirit we must be connected to God. For thousands of years, Christians have intentionally chosen disciplines to build up their faith. For me, I have not been able to pull off any of the traditional spiritual disciplines in my life. Thankfully, Brother Lawrence has offered me, and maybe you, another way to work out our faith--the practice of the presence of God in every moment of every day. In this season of raising toddlers, maybe the place we can connect with God is in the very act of spending time with our kids and asking God to open our eyes to the ways that He is intimately involved in each and every moment.

I do have to confess: every chapter in this book is me trying to live into something that is not fully developed. I know I said earlier that our words and passions don't count as much as our actions. Each of these things I have shared is something I have tried, failed at, and tried again. While I still haven't mastered any of these things, I am firmly committed to figuring it out.

I love Jesus with all my heart. He has invited me into relationship with my Heavenly Father and given me a new identity. He is in the process of healing and transforming me and developing me into the husband and father He has dreamed for me to be. The more I understand who He is and what He is doing in me and in the world, the more I fall in love with Him.

More than any earthly possession, successful career, or even personal safety, I want my kids to fall in love with Jesus in a way that is unique to them. This means that I must work out my own junk, live authentically in front of them, and use each and every method at my disposal to remind them of the way their Father in Heaven loves them. And when I screw up (which I do often), I confess that to them, and once again get up and try again.

I love the art of trying and failing, and then trying and failing some more. When I look back on my life, the accumulation of all these tryings and failings actually have moved me closer to God, and He is using them to transform me more and more into His image.

May you continue to live into the grace God has for you as you try and fail and try and fail, and try again to connect to the heart of God, reflecting His love towards your children. Tomorrow is a new day, and brings a fresh opportunity to experience the love and presences of God in all things glorious and mundane.

"Because of the Lord's great love we are not consumed, for his compassions never fail. They are new every morning; great is your faithfulness." Lamentations 3:22-23

acknowledgements:

As I put the final touches on this book, I am humbled by the many people who have poured their lives into mine and have contributed to shaping me into the man, father, and writer I am today. This book would never have come into being if it wasn't for my wife. Her love and grace toward me is never ending. Her maturity and intentionality in raising our kids is the fruit of her deep love for Christ and being open to the Spirit continually teaching and transforming her.

I am thankful that I have been a part of several communities of people who are invested in me and my family. They have individually contributed to my spiritual growth, my development as a pastor and writer, and have been invaluable to the nurture of my family. With that being said, I would like to thank:

Ed Hart for being my pastor, my mentor and my friend. I am the man I am today because you took a chance in hiring me, opened your life and family to me, and poured love and wisdom into me and my family. I love you.

Zanne Dailey for being my consultant and friend in this project. Your artistic eye for story combined with your ability to say hard things in love has made this book into what it is today. Thank you for not letting me settle for average, but to pursue excellence! I am honored to be in on the ground floor of **ZD Artist Management** (*zdartistmanagement.com*) and pray that God would continue to your ministry.

Sara Cochran for doing life with my family. Living this out is a challenge, and having another family to wade through this with is a gift. I also wanted to thank you for your cover art. It is slick, fun and captures the essence of this book and the tension we feel. **Sara Cochran Design** always does an amazing and classy job taking rough ideas and transforming them into things of beauty! (sara@cochrans.info)

Marin Covenant Church for allowing me space to grow and mature as a pastor and as a writer. I am honored to work at a church that loves and cares for their staff and desire for all of us to continue to grow into the people God has called us to be. I am blown away at your generosity and commitment to children and students. I am honored to be on your team.

Joanna Quintrell for being my spiritual director and helping me discover the unique way in which God has made me and expanded my spiritual diet. You are a gift!

Amanda Milholland for making my wife, my family, my job, and me better.

Lisa Bogart for putting your money where your mouth is and pushing me to write, and to enjoy the rejection process

My friends who have taken on the job as my mini editors. Your encouragement and eye for details have contributed greatly to the end product of this book.

Jeremy Zach for giving me a chance as a writer. As I was just at the beginning of this writing journey, you put a good word in for me with the Orange blogger team and that has opened up many doors. Thank you for your encouragement and support to me and to my colleagues in ministry.

MOPS (Mothers of Pre Schoolers) for being a safe place for so many moms and wives to wrestle with the difficult issues and amazing blessings that come from having little children at home. It is, hands down, my favorite ministry at our church and I am always honored to come and spend time with you.

Orange for being an incredible resource for the church, for families, and for my family as we strive to help our kids know and love Jesus. It is so easy to feel inadequate and unprepared to do this, but your resources have been a gift.

Jesus Christ for redeeming a bruised and broken person. I am eternally thankful for inviting me into your family and to be called your son. Thank you for entrusting me with a family of my own and for extending grace and mercy to me as I strive to be like you as I father my own children.

about the author:

Benjamin Kerns is the Pastor to Children and Students at Marin Covenant Church. For the past 15 years Ben has been pouring into others, encouraging them to live the full and abundant life that is offered through Christ Jesus. He received his M.Div from Bethel Seminary, and is an ordained pastor in the Evangelical Covenant Church.

Ben serves his denomination as a Youth Ministry Facilitator, coaching and mentoring youth workers. Ben is a regularly invited to speak at camps and conferences. He is an established writer and blogger, contributing to journals and websites, including his own blog, averageyouthministry.com.

Made in the USA
Charleston, SC
31 May 2012